TRANSFORMING
THE INNER MAN

CONTENTS

INTRODUCTION

I N 1906 AT AZUSA Street, the long-prophesied fall of the
Holy Spirit in the latter days began. (See Joel 2:28–29.) Since
then, the miracle of the Holy Spirit's presence has contin-
uously expanded. The Lord is now giving back to the Church the
gifts of Ephesians 4:11—apostles, prophets, evangelists, pastors,
and teachers. Men and women are being raised up to serve in high
places: "A man's gift makes room for him" (Prov. 18:16). Wondrous
giftings are elevating many into prominence. All of that is good and
to be celebrated. But too many rising leaders are falling—some to
immorality, others to pressures in their families and organizations,
and so on. Demonic attacks are increasing.

A great problem is that many leaders are like knights with great
gaping holes in their armor, and Satan knows how to bring just
the right (or wrong) persons and circumstances to bring them
down. Many have not had their "eleven years in Tarsus" as Paul
did. In Tarsus God turned a Pharisee's heart into the great loving
saint who wrote most of the letters in the New Testament. What
has been missing from the Church during this present great
outpouring of God's Spirit is a proper theology and understanding

1

of how believers' hearts are to be sanctified after being born anew. Throughout Church history, disciplines and practices for sanctification and transformation have been developed. Believers knew their conversion did not end the process of change; it began it. But that wisdom has largely been lost to this generation.

What happened was that in America, when the westering movement began, people began to pour across the Alleghenies, seeking land and a better life. Thus, for the first time in modern history, the Church was confronted with a moving populace. People had mostly been stationary, living near their birthplace and attending the same church all their lives. Except for a few Congregationalists and Anabaptists, all were members of state churches, supported by taxes. In America, volunteerism arose—churches had to be supported voluntarily by gifts. Electivism was birthed; for the first time, each one chose (elected) where he would go to church. Space broke down ecclesiastical control. By the time an answer to a problem came back from the mother country, by necessity the situation had long had to be settled. Old ways of doing church would no longer work. Thus, leaders had to devise ways of ministering to a fast-moving populace. One of the most cogent answers became a reduction of the Gospel to its simplest message—frighten sinners into the hands of an angry God and then drive them into the arms of a loving Savior, Jesus. "Sawdust and tears" revivalism was born on the American frontier; evangelistic revival preaching had never existed before. It did bear some good fruit. In the first and second Great Awakenings in America, nearly 60 percent of the populace were converted, and many more heard the claims of the Gospel.

But that reduced Gospel knew nothing of sanctification and transformation after being born anew! Many who heard were called to preach—and therefore also knew nothing of ministry to the hurting hearts of the already believing. John and Charles Wesley knew in part and developed a method of sanctification after conversion, for which the church they founded is called to this day the "Methodist" church. But in the fast-flowing evangelism of the frontier, even that was lost.

Eventually preachers began to claim more for the born-anew experience than Scripture can justify. That's not hard to do, because our salvation experience accomplishes so much: our direction is changed from hell to heaven, our sins are forgiven and guilt is washed away in the blood, our flesh is dealt a deathblow, we are restored to fellowship with the Father and with each other, we are given a new heart, and we are filled with the Holy Spirit. But our conversion does not end the process of being transformed into the loving character of Jesus; it begins it. Revival preachers, however, began to claim that from the moment we receive our Lord, our entire character is changed, and we become totally new creatures. Positionally that is true. But Paul, who above all the other apostles made it clear that we are saved solely by grace, also stated clearly that we must "work out [our] salvation with fear and trembling" (Phil. 2:12), that we receive our salvation (healed and transformed character) as the "outcome of [our] faith" (1 Pet. 1:9), not the beginning. But to the many Christians who only knew a concept of conversion that said they were changed more than in actual fact had yet happened, that biblical fact was lost.

The prevalence of that truncated theology has meant that leaders being raised up today have largely remained unaware of the necessity of bringing their fleshly practices to death on the cross after being born anew. (See Colossians 3:9–10.) A proper doctrine and practice of sanctification and transformation have, therefore, been lost to the modern Church. That is perhaps the greatest reason so many leaders today are falling.

This book, the first of four in this series, intends to fill that gap. We will reveal what are many of the practices in the flesh that need to be brought under the salutary effects of confession, repentance, death on the cross, and rebirth into the new after conversion. We will teach how to recognize habits that died positionally when we received Jesus but have sprung back to life to defile many. (See Hebrews 12:15.) We intend to equip the body of Christ (as in Ephesians 4:11–12) to minister to each other's deep wounds and habits with truly saving grace. We want fervently to reveal how the horrible events of our lives are not totally waste and loss but the very ground of wisdom out of which we will be able to minister to others. Because our Lord suffered and was tempted, He is able to minister to those who suffer and are tempted (Heb. 2:18)—and the same is true of us! Transformation means that Satan has won no victories whatsoever in our lives! This book and the three to follow are designed to make Romans 8:28 a reality in our lives, that all things do work together for good to those who are called according to His purpose.

Truly, "My people are destroyed for lack of knowledge" (Hosea 4:6). Herein are keys of knowledge for the sanctification and transformation of every Christian. It remains for us to take hold and put to work His revelations for setting His people free—after all, it is what He said He came to do: "to proclaim release to the captives, and recovery of sight to the blind, to set free those who are downtrodden" (Luke 4:18). Read on, and become His ministers to the wounded and malformed hearts of His people.

CHAPTER 1

SANCTIFICATION AND TRANSFORMATION

And the very God of peace sanctify you wholly; and I pray
God your whole spirit and soul and body be preserved
blameless unto the coming of our Lord Jesus Christ.

—1 THESSALONIANS 5:23, KJV

TRANSFORMATION—TOTAL TRANSFORMATION—IS possible
for every believer. But the process is not easy, and it will
require continual death and rebirth. For many years, Paula
and I have been prayer ministers, pioneering the field of inner
healing. (We prefer the term "prayer minister" to "counselor"
because our approach is based upon biblical principles and prayer
rather than psychology. While we do employ some psychological
insights, we only do so when they agree with scriptural principles.)
The Lord has opened our eyes to understand that there is a vast
difference between specific sins and the hidden sinful practices in
the flesh that lie at their roots.

Before we begin, however, we need to clarify our usage of the term *flesh*. In this context, we are using it to describe our sinful impulses. This is not to be confused with other ways Scripture uses it to describe the holiness of the human body, as in Genesis 2:23, "This is now bone of my bones and flesh of my flesh." *Flesh* in this verse was created in God's image (Gen. 1:26) and continues to bear His image despite the Fall: "A man...is the *image* and glory of God" (1 Cor. 11:7, emphasis added). In their efforts to deal with sin, too many Christians have lost sight of that meaning of "flesh," making it seem that the body itself, as well as our very humanity, is inherently evil. But since how we are to deal with sin is the major thrust of this book, we will use the term *flesh*, unless otherwise specified, to describe the sinful impulses we have inherited from Adam.

Sins need forgiveness. But our *flesh*, which gives birth to sins, can only be dealt with by our own death on the cross. Forgiveness is done for us solely by Jesus. Death on the cross requires our participation. It isn't enough to pray for forgiveness but fail to call the flesh to death on the cross. Nor is it enough daily to die to self on the cross, repenting for sinful behavior, unless we are aware of how to reach to the heart to accomplish death and rebirth where those sinful practices and behaviors were formed. Total transformation of our hearts cannot be fully realized until we lay the ax to the roots. Roots lie hidden, beneath the surface. I believe that the greatest lack of the Church is in not knowing how to transform our hearts at the deep level of *causes*, dealing with sins and inclination toward sin. Without dealing at the level of roots, true sanctification and transformation cannot be fully accomplished in the body of Christ.

We have all been like little children, fumbling unwittingly with the key to the door of sanctification. "See to it that no one comes short of the grace of God; that no *root* of bitterness springing up causes trouble, and by it many be defiled" (Heb. 12:15, emphasis added). We must comprehend that the full vision of inner transformation can only be accomplished by *continual* death and rebirth. God does not want only to restore men to the abundant life (John 10:10). He also wants to raise perfected sons.

The ministry to the inner man is not merely a tool to heal a *few troubled* individuals; it is a vital key to the transformation of *every* heart of *every normal* Christian! In this book I want to help you understand that transformation will require more than just accepting Christ as Lord and Savior. I want to help you learn to apply the cross of Christ through prayer and counsel to sinful structures built into your heart over a lifetime. Because, although every sinful deed was fully washed away when you accepted Jesus as your Lord, not every part of your heart was immediately able to fully appropriate the good news of that fact.

> Take care, brethren, lest there should be in any one of you an evil, *unbelieving heart,* in falling away from the living God.
> —HEBREW 3:12, EMPHASIS ADDED

We will take a close look at sound biblical and evangelical understandings of our flesh, as well as consider important psychological teachings. Psychology, insofar as it follows its founders' teachings, proposes that life writes on us who we are, that we are conditioned by what happens *to* us. It tends to overlook sin and talk about conditioning, thus minimizing guilt. Sound theology maintains that many practices in us stem from our flesh itself, quite apart causally from events in this life. As Christians, we believe that what is already in us by inheritance from Adam colors our interpretation of all that happens to us and influences drastically our choices in responding. Further, Adamic sin often inclines us toward wrong choices before events begin to form us wrongly (more on this later). It is not merely that life does things to us; we first do some things to life.

Psychologists want to restore the individual to a functioning level; Christians want to forgive and bring to death and rebirth. In this book, I want the believer who wants to experience total transformation to understand how God matures a soul. We will look to the entire life, especially to the transformation of the flesh. I will show you steps for reaching to the depths of your heart with the power of the cross and resurrection so you can effect lasting change by continual death and rebirth.

DEALING WITH THE HEART

For many years I had pondered the question of the Church's continuing perversity and weakness despite the presence of the Word, the Holy Spirit, and the gifts. I saw that one major missing element in the Church's life and ministry is its lack of comprehension of the necessity and ways of inner sanctification and transformation. In short, the heart has never yet been effectively dealt with. "They have healed the brokenness of My people superficially, saying, 'Peace, peace,' but there is no peace" (Jer. 6:14; see also Jer. 8:11).

Scripture passages began to leap out at me:

> The Spirit of the Lord is upon Me, because He anointed Me to preach the gospel to the poor. He has sent Me to proclaim release to the captives, and *recovery of sight* to the blind, *to set free* those who are downtrodden, to proclaim the favorable year of the Lord.
>
> —LUKE 4:18–19, EMPHASIS ADDED

> And do not be *conformed* to this world, but be *transformed* by the renewing of your mind, that you may prove what the will of God is, that which is good and acceptable and perfect.
>
> —ROMANS 12:2, EMPHASIS ADDED

> *Put to death your members which are on the earth: fornication, uncleanness, passion, evil desire, and covetousness, which is idolatry....* Do not lie to one another, since you have *put off* the old man with his deeds.
>
> —COLOSSIANS 3:5, 9, NKJV, EMPHASIS ADDED

And so, as those who have been chosen of God, holy and beloved, *put on* a heart of compassion, kindness, humility, gentleness, and patience.

—COLOSSIANS 3:12, EMPHASIS ADDED

See to it that no one comes short of the grace of God; that no *root of bitterness* springing up causes trouble, and by it many be defiled.

—HEBREWS 12:15, EMPHASIS ADDED

Woe to you, scribes and Pharisees, hypocrites! For you clean the *outside* of the cup and of the dish, but *inside* they are full of robbery and self-indulgence. You blind Pharisee, first *clean the inside* of the cup and of the dish, so that the outside of it may become clean also.

—MATTHEW 23:25–26, EMPHASIS ADDED

And like living stones *be yourselves built* into a spiritual house, to be a holy priesthood, to offer spiritual sacrifices acceptable to God through Jesus Christ. For it stands in scripture: "Behold, I am laying in Zion a stone, a cornerstone chosen and precious, and he who believes in him will not be put to shame."

—1 PETER 2:5–6, RSV, EMPHASIS ADDED

I understood then that the Holy Spirit intended to open a door to ministry for the entire body of Christ. It was not merely for a few superstars to heal a few troubled ones, but for the sanctification and maturation of every member of the body, done by Him, *by all, for all.* He did not want only to heal specific memories, nor did He want merely to forgive particular sins. He purposed to raise up a John-the-Baptist ministry to lay the ax to *every* root of *every* tree (Luke 3:9). He is raising up His "messenger" to purify the entire Church, and through it, the world: "And He will sit as a smelter and purifier of silver, and He will purify the sons of Levi and refine them like gold and silver, so that they may present to the LORD offerings in righteousness" (Mal. 3:3).

> To me, the very least of all saints, this grace was given, to preach to the Gentiles the unfathomable riches of Christ, and to bring to light what is the administration of the mystery which for ages has been hidden in God, who created all things; in order that the manifold *wisdom of God might now be made known through the church* to the rulers and the authorities in the heavenly places.
>
> —EPHESIANS 3:8–10, EMPHASIS ADDED

Overeager and overzealous, I tried to write this vision for the body of Christ. That was in the winter of 1968–1969 in Wallace, Idaho. From November to March, snow lay more than six feet deep! I was writing on sheets of paper laid out on a table in our camper. Returning from a speaking mission, I discovered that the weight of melting snow had sprung a leak in the camper roof, in only one place—directly over my worktable! Everything was soaked. The lines of writing were blurred on every page, and all the pages were stuck together. How much better could the Lord have proclaimed, "John, you're all wet!"

Then came the "seven years of eating grass," of which we wrote in *The Elijah Task,* chapter four. During that time I was to see a major correction in my thinking—like turning the world upside down (Acts 17:6)! My picture of transformation could then have been represented by the frame of a man in which crosses could be superimposed upon sores here and there until the entire man was cleansed and became whole. I thought that as the Lord transformed one area of trouble after another, we would become better and better, holier and holier, until at last we arrived at the perfect man, which I thought had been promised in Ephesians 4:15–16.

Slaying the Power of Control

I was to see in those seven years of suffering that the Holy Spirit does *not* intend to improve us or make us better and better! He intends to bring us to fullness of death and make us new. I learned also that transforming the inner man does not once and for all fully reform our flesh this side of physical death, *but rather it slays its power to control us,* while clothing us with the righteousness of Jesus. *"He* is the source of your life in Christ Jesus, whom God made our wisdom, our righteousness and sanctification and redemption" (1 Cor. 1:30, RSV, emphasis added). If, on this side of mankind's ultimate perfection, the Holy Spirit were to so transform any area of a man's flesh that he could always rely on the supposed righteousness of that dimension of his character, that man would inevitably cease to lean on Jesus and begin to trust in his own flesh. His perfection would thus have to be total, or he could not escape the corruption of pride. He would lose gratitude for Jesus' continuing salvation. Therefore, the Lord so heals that we may have confidence and rest, but only in *His ability* to keep us, not in the strength of *our* character or *our* will to do right. Paradoxically, we are healed by being taught to put no confidence whatsoever in our own flesh, simply to rest in Him. The permanence of our change is in His steadfastness, not something supposedly solidly built or changed in us except a fresh ability to trust in Him. "For we are the true circumcision, who worship in the Spirit of God and glory in Christ Jesus *and put no confidence in the flesh"* (Phil. 3:3, emphasis added).

It became clear to me that since many Christian counselors, rightly using psychological insights, had wrongly taken their stand in psychology's basic assumptions, much confusion was resulting. Psychologists would mend our self-images so that we could have confidence *in ourselves.* But Christ would slay all our fleshly self-confidence so that our only self-image becomes, "I can do all things *through Him* who strengthens me" (Phil. 4:13, emphasis added). A self-image is something *we* build, in which we falsely learn to trust.

A self-image necessarily sets us into self-centered striving—to live up to it and to make sure others see and reward it; we must defend it, build and rebuild it, and so on. But a Christian's identity is a gift, something God builds in us, not having to be seen, rewarded, or defended.

True healing comes, then, not by making a broken thing good enough to work, but by delivering us from the power of that broken thing so that it can no longer rule us and by teaching us to trust *His* righteousness to shine in and through that very thing. Those who heal by restoring the self-image cause people to trust in something repaired in the flesh, merely reshaping their old carnal practices, which sooner or later dooms them to failure, whereas the Lord heals by leaving the broken part right there in place, overcoming it by His nature. Our trust as Christians can only be in His righteousness in us and for us—always!

Thus the world is turned upside down! The world would fix the broken thing and rebuild personal pride and confidence. The Lord says, "We'll fix it by not mending it at all! We'll use that broken thing to give glory to God, and from that awareness of sin we will build a trust every day anew in God's Holy Spirit to sing the beauty of Christ's nature through us for all to see." We do not have to say, "We'll be careful to give You all the glory." Once we fully understand our death in sin, He already has it all! *We* do no good thing. *He* accomplishes all. Thus, for the soul, there is in that sense no "healing"— only death and rebirth. The Old Testament does speak of restoring the soul (Ps. 23:3; 19:7; etc.), but Christians need continually to translate that to mean by death and rebirth in Jesus' righteousness.

> Therefore we have been buried with Him through baptism into death, in order that as Christ was raised from the dead through the glory of the Father, so we too might walk in newness of life. For if we have become united with Him in the likeness of His death, certainly we shall be also in the likeness of His resurrection, knowing this, that our old self was crucified with Him,

that our body of sin might be done away with, that we should no longer be slaves to sin; for he who has died is freed from sin. Now if we have died with Christ, we believe that we shall also live with Him.

—ROMANS 6:4–8

At precisely this theological turning point many professional counselors have driven people's ships upon the rocks. Whoever seeks to rebuild another's self-image (apart from Christ in us) works against the cross.

Those who desire to make a good showing in the flesh try to compel you to be circumcised, simply that they may not be persecuted for the cross of Christ.... But may it never be that I should boast, except in the cross of our Lord Jesus Christ, through which the world has been crucified to me, and I to the world.

—GALATIANS 6:12–14

We suggest that for "be circumcised," the reader substitute "find and live for your own self-image," rereading these verses in that light.

All this could sound as though we ought not, in the world or in Christ, attempt to build good character. "It's all doomed to fail anyway, so why try?" Though God may destroy that which we have built apart from Him, He never discourages our own character-building attempts. "First the blade, then the head, then the mature grain in the head" (Mark 4:28). God knows that the sooner and the harder we try, the earlier we shall discover our need of a Savior. He knows that when what *we* have built ripens to disgust, it and we will fall to death, and then whatever was of wood, hay, or stubble will be burnt up in the fire—leaving in the process the trace of wisdom that will enable Him to build us anew with stone and silver and gold (1 Cor. 3:11–15). So God loves a stable home that builds solidly in the soul. Though He can and does turn failure to glory, how much more He prefers to turn a beautifully formed character to death and rebirth, for then it has not only the glory of wisdom but also the beauty of the ages in its inheritance.

SANCTIFICATION

Good or bad, whatever of character is built in us must come to death and reformation in Christ. Sanctification is not a process of removing each spot of corrupt practices until the whole nature shines as something beautiful (as I had thought). Far from seeing ourselves as able to achieve perfection, we need to remember that we have this "treasure in earthen vessels" (2 Cor. 4:7), and we have come to rest about that in Jesus.

At the end of St. Paul's ministry, when men took handkerchiefs from his body and laid them on the sick, they recovered (Acts 19:12). St. Paul wrote: "It is a trustworthy statement, deserving full acceptance, that Christ Jesus came into the world to save sinners, among whom I *am foremost of all*" (1 Tim. 1:15, emphasis added). It was not that St. Paul had been a sinner and was now an innocent saint. Maturity had meant instead an increasing awareness of *present sin* until he knew himself to be the chief of sinners! In effect, he was saying, "I haven't arrived yet. I still think I'm better than *some* people!" His was a progression from knowing himself as having sinned worthy of death to realizing that his death was already a *fact* because of his sins: "Even when we were *dead* in our transgressions, [God] made us alive together with Christ (by grace you have been saved)" (Eph. 2:5, emphasis added). St. Paul saw that Jesus Christ did not merely die for *sins* but for *sin.* We are not merely sinners. Every part of our being has become infected with sin! As Pogo said so eloquently, "We have met the enemy—and they is us!" "For I know that *nothing good* dwells in me, that is, in my flesh; for the wishing is present in me, but the doing of the good is not" (Rom. 7:18, emphasis added). "He made Him who knew no sin to be sin on our behalf, that we might become the righteousness of God in Him" (2 Cor. 5:21). The result of such comprehension of the depth of our sin is that His nature outshines and glories through all our brokennesses.

Jesus became not only the perfect sacrifice for our *sins*, but He also became like us in every respect (Heb. 2:14–16). Since the fall of Adam and Eve, sin is our overpowering inclination. That is what Jesus became and what He died for. His was not merely a physical death on the cross. Having become our sin in all that He was, He died in all that He was—heart, mind, soul, and body. It is from that fullness of death that Jesus raises us to be new creatures in Him. Truly we *are* new creatures. "Therefore if any man is in Christ, he is a new creature; the old things passed away; behold, new things have come" (2 Cor. 5:17).

Nevertheless, a danger remains. We may forget that underneath the glorious new robe of Jesus, the rust of our own corruption waits to reassert itself the moment we turn away from Him.

We would like to feel, after all, that we are pretty good people. To be sure, we did some awful things. But Jesus paid the price for that, and now we can be the "good guys" God created us to be. Not that way, folks! You can't peel it off and get down to the good. The whole thing got infected, and now it's "leave it there, and put on Him" (Col. 3). That is how we have the new nature: by wearing it.

What the Church has lacked is day-by-day death and rebirth in Christ. We have smugly sung that death and rebirth have been accomplished when the process has only begun! The very saint who wrote that salvation is a free gift not of works (Eph. 2:8–9) also wrote, "*Work* out your salvation with fear and trembling" (Phil. 2:12, emphasis added). The *blood* of Jesus washes away sins, and the *cross* redeems, justifies, and atones, while His *resurrection* restores and gives new life. But it is our personal daily taking up of *our own cross* that continues the necessary slaughter of our old man. Only as that daily work of continuing sanctification happens to the fullest does the mature man of faith appear, whether that be an individual or the corporate body of Christ (Eph. 4:16). From birth on, each of us is trying to build a self we can accept. It is the same striving, no matter whether we want to be like God, gentle and good, or powerful or evil. The attempt is to build a character structure that works the way we want it to. All too many Christians, without being aware of it, are still trying to *use* the Lord to build that good self. Their prayers and deeds are to that end. But that is not the Lord's design. He does not want us to build a successful self. That whole search to build something we can accept and rest in is the very thing that was to have died on the cross. Continuing to try to build ourselves is actually based on flight from accepting what we are—as though if we could just build something powerful or lovely enough, we might come to peace about ourselves and forget the search to overcome the hidden rottenness in our core. But the simple good news is that the search is already ended. We are already accepted, right where we are, as we are. The Lord's love is unconditional. *He* will build us.

The Lord wants us to accept ourselves as we are, rotten and unchanged, and then let Him express His goodness and righteousness in us through His Holy Spirit. "And coming to Him as to a living stone, rejected by men, but choice and precious in the sight of God, you also, as living stones, are *being built up* as a spiritual house for a holy priesthood, to offer up spiritual sacrifices acceptable to God through Jesus Christ" (1 Pet. 2:4–5, emphasis added). Note the passive voice: "being built," not "build yourselves." The call is not to build; the call is to die.

> I urge you therefore, brethren, by the mercies of God, to present your bodies a living and holy sacrifice, acceptable to God, which is your spiritual service of worship. And do not be conformed to this world, but be transformed by the renewing of your mind, that you may prove what the will of God is, that which is good and acceptable and perfect.
>
> —ROMANS 12:1–2

And He was saying to them all, "If anyone wishes to come after Me, let him deny himself, and take up his cross daily, and follow Me."

—LUKE 9:23

I have been crucified with Christ; and it is no longer I who live, but Christ lives in me: and the life which I now live in the flesh I live by faith in the Son of God, who loved me, and delivered Himself up for me.

—GALATIANS 2:20

Now those who belong to Christ Jesus have crucified the flesh with its passions and desires.

—GALATIANS 5:24

The tragedy is that too many Christians are still trying to build rather than to rest in Him. Sanctification is the process by which we come to rest in Him. Sanctification is daily death and rebirth. Sanctification is that part of the maturation of the sons of God that proceeds by the Holy Spirit solely through the cross of Christ, borne individually! The end product of sanctification is not only a new person but also a clean one. "Now in a large house there are not only gold and silver vessels, but also vessels of wood and of earthenware, and some to honor and some to dishonor. Therefore, if a man cleanses himself from these things, he will be a vessel for honor, sanctified, useful to the Master, and prepared for every good work" (2 Tim. 2:20–21).

Before the Fall, sanctification and maturation were one and the same—steady, simple growth in humility into the holy wisdom of God, just as Jesus "increased in wisdom and stature, and in favour with God and man" (Luke 2:52, KJV), yet without sin. The fall of man, descending from generation to generation (Deut. 5:9), demands death and rebirth.

In every age, God's work has been to raise His sons. Sin being what it is, ever since Adam and Eve He has always been about the business of changing hearts. Healing of the inner man is not new; we only call the process by new names. The new fact is that today God is calling the entire indwelt body of Christ to ministry and maturity. Maturity comes by the Word and sanctification. Sanctification happens as Christians learn to speak the truth to one another in love (Eph. 4:15).

TRANSFORMATION

Transformation is that process of death and rebirth whereby what was our weakness becomes our strength. Sanctification overcomes the power of canceled sin, but transformation turns the mess to glory. As is true for the work of inner healing, so transformation of the inner man is not the work of a few superstars. It is the labor of the entire body of Christ, in labor pains for the continual birth of the body: "My children, with whom I am again in labor until Christ is formed in you" (Gal. 4:19). Transformation is the work of the total body of Christ to prepare us all as a bride adorned for her husband.

Transformation proceeds by brokenness: "The LORD is near to the brokenhearted, and saves those who are crushed in spirit" (Ps. 34:18). Wherein we still trust in our own righteousness, His grace has little room to express His righteousness. But wherein we are acutely aware of our sin and brokenness, His life is most set free to be resurrection life in us. Truly our "strength is made perfect in weakness" (2 Cor. 12:9, KJV).

The good news of the Gospel is not merely pardon, which leaves the record of sin and of itself says nothing of change in the sinner. (In legal terms, *pardon* only says that the sinner will no longer be punished, whereas *forgiveness* erases the record of sin.) The good news is justification (that in Christ the debt ledger is paid and we are even with the board again). The good news is also, but not merely, redemption, that in Christ Jesus we are bought back from the hand of death. The good news is victorious fulfillment! We do not only get out of jail free, but we also pass GO and collect $200 with all our mortgages paid and houses and hotels collecting rent again!

It is not as though we started from ground zero on a scale of one to ten, arrived at point two, and fell, being subsequently returned by grace to point two to begin again. It is as though having fallen at two, we have returned as the prodigal son at point seven or more to put on the ring and robe of authority, having gained by what we have been through, wiser and richer than we would have been had we never fallen—even as the heart of the prodigal son knew more of his father's love than his elder brother did (Luke 15:11–32).

It is not merely that our waste places are comforted. Every wilderness in our personal life becomes part of the tree of life of Revelation 22:2, "for the healing of the nations." Our deserts are turned to glorious gardens for the feeding of others. That is the joy of the Gospel and the meaning of transformation: not merely return, but fullness of victory for ministry to others.

Grace never says that we should run out to sin in order to become wiser. Rather, as awful as sin is and as much as it is to be deplored, the latter side of it by the foolishness of the Gospel is the grace of God to turn every worst degradation into our highest glory! Some have naively said what is not in God's Word: "If you haven't forgotten, you haven't forgiven," and "You should forget you ever sinned." Far from forgetting our sins, we are to remember them with sweet gratitude and joy. God "forgets" our sin, but this does not mean God develops amnesia. Rather, He "forgets" by no longer counting our sins against us. Our forgetting should be akin to His. Having fallen, remembering means we cannot justify blaming another, and we are prepared by our "misbeings" and "misdoings" to help others from the same holes and traps.

TRANSFORMED TO MINISTER

Therein is the specific meaning of the word *transformation*. Death and rebirth alone could seem to connote that the old was all a waste and should not have been at all, and that the new creature has no relation to it whatsoever. But transformation rises out of, "For since He Himself was tempted in that which He has suffered, He is able to come to the aid of those who are tempted" (Heb. 2:18). Because of where we have been, we are able to minister. The new creature in Christ now treasures the lessons learned through struggling with the old man. If he does not appreciate who he has become in Christ and still shudders in shame, transformation is not yet complete, for in the failures and corruptions of the old the gold of wisdom was formed, "tried in a furnace on the earth, refined seven times" (Ps. 12:6).

> Blessed be the God and Father of our Lord Jesus Christ, the Father of mercies and God of all comfort; who comforts us in all our affliction so that we may be able to comfort those who are in any affliction with the comfort with which we ourselves are comforted by God. For just as the sufferings of Christ are ours in abundance, so also our comfort is abundant through Christ. But if we are afflicted, it is for your comfort and salvation; or if we are comforted, it is for your comfort, which is effective in the patient enduring of the same sufferings which we also suffer; and our hope for you is firmly grounded, knowing that as you are sharers of our sufferings, so also you are sharers of our comfort.
>
> —2 CORINTHIANS 1:3–7

A pearl is one of the symbols of wisdom because wisdom is formed in the same way a pearl is formed. A grain of sand becomes an irritant, forcing the oyster to wrap layers of pearl around it. Likewise the irritant of sin, crucified and coated with the blood and righteousness of Jesus, writes into our hearts a wisdom priceless beyond rubies (Jer. 31:33; Prov. 3:15; 8:11).

"Healing of memories," as taught by some, seems to say that we should erase the old. Neither true healing nor transformation ever erases what is past. That would be to invalidate rather than to celebrate. Transformation says, "For this reason we have lived and sinned and have been redeemed, that out of the ashes of what we have been and have done has grown the ministry we are," which is why we prefer not to use the term *healing of memories*.

Transformation holds implicit that nothing in our lives is ever wasted. The prevenient grace of God is so complete that there is no event in our lives without which we would be better off. Transformation, therefore, confirms that Satan has won no victories whatsoever among the saved, for from the ground plan of Creation, even as God planned to turn the lowly cross to highest victory, so He has turned *every* aspect of our (seemingly) defeated lives to glory!

As C. S. Lewis wrote in his book *The Great Divorce*, transformation celebrates that the lizard that rode our backs is the very thing that will become the noble steed to carry us to victory in the battle for others. Transformed alcoholics minister best to alcoholics. The formerly depressed know by their own desert experiences how to feed the downtrodden the only kind of manna they can receive. The judgmental become tenderhearted extenders of mercy. Hearts of stone become warm hearts of flesh to melt wintry souls (Ezek. 36:26).

Transformation is, therefore, not synonymous with healing (unless we mean by "healing" what transformation truly is). The word *healing* seems to imply that something that formerly worked became broken, so we fix it. In our carnal thinking formed in the world, healing may yet mean "to restore something formerly good to working order again"—like a good car with some hidden flaw, which creates a malfunction until a mechanic discovers and fixes it. That's fine. Good things need to be mended. But that analogy cannot be applied to the human soul. To the body, yes. Our bodies are good and clean, washed by the blood of Jesus (Acts 10:15), and often need to be mended. But no structure in our flesh is to be patched up; every part is to be slain and reborn. The human soul is not in that sense to be mended: "But no one puts a patch of unshrunk cloth on an old garment; for the patch pulls away from the garment, and a worse tear results. Nor do men put new wine into old wineskins; otherwise the wineskins burst, and the wine pours out, and the wineskins are ruined; but they put new wine into fresh wineskins, and both are preserved" (Matt. 9:16–17). The inner being is not inclined toward moral goodness, that it should be restored: "For I know that nothing good dwells in me, that is, in my flesh; for the wishing is present in me, but the doing of the good is not" (Rom. 7:18).

We died and were made perfect, positionally, in every part of us, when we first received Jesus as Lord and Savior: "For by one offering He has perfected for all time those who are sanctified" (Heb. 10:14). Abraham was given the land of Canaan when he first arrived there (Gen. 15:7–21), but it took centuries of suffering, imprisonment, exodus, trials, wilderness-walking, and conquering before the Israelites did, in fact, possess what was already positionally theirs. Just so, our total being received its deathblow at the moment of our conversion. That innermost salvation must become manifest in our lives in entirety (Phil. 2:12). But our entire selves are not always aware of or ready for death and rebirth! By common sense, this side of death, we simply could not stand to be completely transformed all in one moment. The Lord intends to *put* His laws in our minds and to *write* them on our hearts (Jer. 31:33; Heb. 8:10). That *writing* lasts a painful while (1 Pet. 5:6–10). It requires a slow process. That is one reason for the church and, within the church, for the ministry of small groups (or cell groups). As we were not naturally born and raised by ourselves, without fathers and mothers, so spiritually we are not slain and reborn without the ministry of the body of Christ. Though the body may err, Christ will use those very errors to inscribe lessons on our hearts, and He will not fail.

This book is written to inform the Church for ministry. God has placed us within the Church for this reason, that through the Church He may transform our flesh:

> ...for the equipping of the saints for the work of service, to the building up of the body of Christ; until we all attain to the unity of the faith, and of the knowledge of the Son of God, to a mature man, to the measure of the stature which belongs to the fulness of Christ. As a result, we are no longer to be children, tossed here and there by waves, and carried about by every wind of doctrine, by the trickery of men, by craftiness in deceitful scheming; but speaking the truth in love, we are to grow up in all aspects into Him, who is the head, even Christ, from whom the whole body, being fitted and held together by that which every joint supplies, according to the proper working of each individual part, causes the growth of the body for the building up of itself in love.
>
> —EPHESIANS 4:12–16

CHAPTER 2

SEEING GOD WITH AN UNBELIEVING HEART

> Take heed, brethren, lest there be in any of you an evil heart of unbelief, in departing from the living God.
>
> —HEBREWS 3:12, KJV

THE PROBLEM OF BELIEF in God has never been solely to convince the conscious mind. If it were, He would need only to raise up forensic debaters or brilliant apologists rather than pastors and churches who nurture. "For with the *heart* man believeth unto righteousness; and with the mouth confession is made unto salvation" (Rom. 10:10, KJV, emphasis added). It seems to me that too often we have all mentally mistranslated the passage: "For with the *mind* man comes to believe, and confesses with his mouth." It is easy to confuse deep, heartfelt conviction with mere intellectual assent and to think salvation is thereby accomplished. I do not mean to say that anyone's conversion experience is thereby invalid, but that it did not finish the process. We have been too easily convinced of completion.

The Unbelieving Heart of a Believer

When belief in the heart, to whatever degree, opens the floodgates of understanding to the mind and conviction to the spirit, and we respond in the sinner's prayer to invite Jesus in, we *are* redeemed. That is an eternally accomplished fact. In that moment, we *are* justified, a thing needing never to be repeated by us or by the Lord. Our sins are washed away in the blood of the Lamb. Our destiny is changed from hell to heaven. We are once and for all time fully "saved."

But that experience of conversion is not all there is to being saved. Christians use the word *salvation* too loosely. Salvation is a far larger word than justification or redemption or being born anew or going to heaven, or all these and more put together. Redemption and justification are entrances to the process of growing into salvation (1 Pet. 2). So also is being born anew. Going to heaven is the end product. All of what happens in between, the process of sanctification and transformation, is the major part of salvation, which means etymologically from its root, "to become whole, to be healed."

When we ask, "Have you been saved, brother?" we mean "redeemed," "justified," "born anew," and "going to heaven." Well and good. Perhaps there are no better words to use. But the question is confusing. If we mean, "Has the Lord gotten hold of you, paid the price, and set your face toward heaven?" every born-anew Christian ought to answer with an unqualified, "Yes, I'm saved, and I'm going to heaven." But concerning the *process in this life* of *being* saved, none ought ever to reply that it is all done. Each one should answer, "I'm saved, and I'm being saved every day," because "by one offering He has perfected for all time those who are sanctified" (Heb. 10:14).

The question is further confounded by the fact that though every believer is in process, he knows by faith (as we said earlier) that *positionally* he has already been made perfect (Heb. 10:14) and is already being raised up to sit with Him in heavenly places (Eph. 2:6). "It is finished" (John 19:30). Perhaps we will have to continue using "saved" and "salvation" when we actually mean only "converted." But for our purpose here (to reveal the process of sanctification and transformation and our part in it), whatever *further* conversions of the heart we explore ought never to be taken to imply that our first conversion was invalid or insufficient for entrance to heaven. On the other hand, no matter how dramatic or conclusive that conversion was, we run the risk of crippling our abundant life and further salvation the moment we "build a tabernacle" as though it once and for all finished the process it, in fact, only began. The heart needs to be transformed anew in far more reaching areas every day, or we fail to grow in Jesus. Indeed, that is our primary definition of growth in Christ—further and further death and rebirth through *continuing* inner conversion.

One might ask, "Isn't it confusing to insist that we need to be converted anew when we have already been converted?" It may be, but we don't know a better way to say it.

Continual conversion of a believer's heart, which moves the heart from a place of unbelief to a place of belief and repentance, can take place as a believer places himself or herself under the ministry of the preaching and teaching of faith for repentance and conversion. As the light of God's Word reaches into the dark, hidden recesses of the heart, "plowing" up the stubborn clods of self-righteousness and weeding out the old in mind and heart, the heart is prepared to produce good fruit, sixty to a hundredfold (Matt. 13:3–8). The sword of truth pierces "even to the dividing asunder of soul and spirit, and of the joints and marrow, and is a discerner of the thoughts and intents of the heart" (Heb. 4:12, KJV). Note carefully: "the thoughts and intents *of the heart*," not the conscious mind. Thus the *primary* task of a small group leader is that of an evangelist, bringing the Gospel by circumstances and counsel to the unbelieving heart of the already believing. Evangelism of the unbelieving hearts of believers is the continuing and constant work of small group leaders; indeed, evangelism is the primary way of all sanctification and transformation.

In the first and second Great Awakenings in America, many evangelists arose, and Congregationalists in New England were converted by the thousands. The converted then asked, "What's next?" and began to say, "We need to grow up." The results of their pioneering efforts in Christian education were the founding of Sunday schools, public schools, and many of our great colleges—Harvard, Yale, Dartmouth, Oberlin, Yankton, Drury, and so on. But Congregationalists lacked sufficient awareness of the need for the heart to be continually converted. After a while, the denomination lost sight of the need for conversion altogether! Other evangelists appeared, crying for repentance and rebirth. Many who responded to their preaching never heard the call to mature or, like the Congregationalists, tried to mature but missed the essential element of continual death and rebirth in the inner man.

Therefore, historically in America, sanctification came to mean striving to live up to the law upon the base of a supposedly already transformed character. That struggle all too often led to judgmentalism and hypocrisy rather than to the gentle nature of Jesus. It led to Phariseeism, thus "Puritanism," against which many Americans still rebel today. Part of the tragic misunderstanding was that the *transformation* had never been *that* complete. True, we are washed clean at the moment of conversion (though we may need to be cleaned again and again). And so are our consciences sprinkled (Heb. 9:14). But not all the character has been transformed.

The maturation of the entire Church waits upon this laying down of the foundation for transformation. Jesus is not yet that firmly seated as Lord in the inner depths of most Christians. It must hurt the Lord deeply that in churches considered most sound doctrinally and evangelically, even in those churches most filled with the Holy Spirit, sin so often still runs rampant, even among the leaders! Or even where obvious sin has not reared its head, so little fruit of the Spirit is seen. Or if His fruit is there, battles and dissensions seem never far away. In such churches conversion may be complete in the conscious mind, but in the *heart* (from which comes evil) the fields remain "white already to harvest"—and almost untouched!

The Lord must be allowed to occupy the "land" of inner space in each believer's heart. This will be accomplished through the weapon of the Word of God being spoken to one another through the preaching of the Word, through the ministry of small groups, and through diligent, intercessory prayer for and with each other—not by psychological cleverness or analysis. As the Word touches the places of unbelief in our hearts, we will arise in conversion to take up the battle cry against the flesh and make it our joy to plunge to inner death and rebirth.

How We See God

> Blessed are the pure in heart: for they shall see God.
> —MATTHEW 5:8, KJV

Mark again those words, "pure *in heart.*" I (John) used to think that since I had received Jesus, I would someday (when I died) be allowed to see God the Father and be unafraid when that time came. Of course that is true, but the Lord has been revealing that to "see" God does not refer so much to physical sight as to come to know and comprehend His nature. In conversation we say, "Oh, I see," when we really mean, "I understand." Jesus was saying that those whose hearts are purified come to understand and embrace God for who He actually is. The inference is that because our hearts are not pure, we impute to God motives and ways that are not His. We do not see God, but only our projection of Him.

"We love, because He first loved us. If some one says, 'I love God,' and hates his brother, he is a liar; for the one who does not love his brother whom he has seen, cannot love God whom he has not seen. And this commandment we have from Him, that the one who loves God should love his brother also" (1 John 4:19–21). Here we see that the impurity is hate. Hate blinds the eyes. We are told further that our hatred of fellow human beings colors what we see of God—or prevents it altogether; we do not love or see God. That is one of the primary facts that necessitate continual conversion of the heart. Our hidden and forgotten judgments, especially against our fathers and mothers, prevent us from seeing God as He is.

"He who curses his father or his mother, his lamp will go out in time of darkness" (Prov. 20:20). We call this our "20/20 vision scripture." Our judgments made against our parents in childhood, usually long forgotten, have darkened our spiritual eyes. We do not see ourselves, others, life, or God with 20/20 vision. "The spirit of man is the lamp of the LORD, searching all the innermost parts of his being" (v. 27). Our lamp fails to discern our own hidden ways, or those of others, to the degree and in the areas in which judgments have been made and our spirits have been consequently darkened.

People have many times come to us saying, "Don't talk to me about a loving God. Why doesn't He stop all the wars, or at least prevent some of the bestial things men do to men, sometimes in the very name of religion? Or doesn't He care?" We have all heard statements like that. Being prayer ministers, Paula and I never try to defend God. We avoid theological debates (1 Tim. 6:20). We know the answer is not a mental one but a matter of an impure heart. We merely ask, "What was your father like?"

Invariably we uncover a history similar to what the person has imputed to God—cruelty, insensitivity, desertion, criticism, and so forth. No matter what the *mind* may learn in Sunday school of a gentle and loving God who "so loved the world, that He gave His only begotten Son" (John 3:16), the *heart* has been scarred and shaped by reactions to our earthly fathers. As a result, we often project cruelty, insensitivity, desertion, criticism, and other negative factors onto our understanding of who God is. Our minds may declare His goodness, but our behaviors reveal what the heart really thinks: "As [a man] thinks in his heart, so is he" (Prov. 23:7, NKJV).

Until we are able to forgive our natural fathers for the hurts they may have caused in our hearts and repent for the judgments we have formed against them, we will not be able to truly see God as gentle, kind, and lovingly present in our lives.

THE ROOTS OF UNBELIEF

Paula had a wonderful father who was kind and strong, witty and sensitive. But he was a traveling salesman on the road two or three weeks at a time. The mind of the little girl thought, *I love my daddy; I'm proud of him. He goes to work for us.* But her hidden heart was not that magnanimous. It was saying, "Why isn't he ever here for me, and why is everything more important than I am?" Her heart was angrily making resolves: "I'll have to do everything for myself. No one will be here to defend me."

Paula received the Lord when she was eleven and thereafter knew God as a loving heavenly Father (perhaps more easily because her father was). Secretly, however, part of her was cherishing bitterness and could not believe that God would be there twenty-four hours a day, three hundred sixty-five days a year. On weekends, because her father had been home and had gone to church with the family, she could feel close to God, especially in the fellowship of worship. But during the week, despite what her mind grasped of Psalms 91 and 121, she could not sense as reality that God was there for her. Because of her sinful hidden reactions to her weekend father, hers was a "weekend God." Finally, at my insistence, though she never had nor ever has felt any resentment toward her father, she gambled that something must be there (1 Cor. 4:4) and repented solely by faith. God answered by immediate changes in many of her mental attitudes, especially toward me, and then wrote upon her heart His capacity to protect her in a most dramatic way. But let Paula tell it herself.

John and I were on our way to Seattle, Washington, to minister to a group of Christian counselors. It was a beautiful day, and I was at the wheel of our new car. I had often been very critical of John's reluctance to give up the driver's seat even when he was drowsy, but this day he had relinquished his position with admirable grace and trust. The cruise control was set at fifty-five miles per hour, the car radio was playing quietly, John was nodding toward a nap, and I was relaxed and confident as we headed west on the highway.

The next thing I knew, I was being jostled awake by John's elbow in my ribs. I looked out the left window and saw the road going by, level with the top of the window! On the right, I could see nothing but rocky hillside at close range. Stretching ahead of us was a gravel-filled ditch, and we were running through it! But in that instant all my awareness and responses seemed to be in a great calm, quiet, unbelievable slow motion. No butterflies. No panic. Just profound silence.

We have gone off the road into a deep ditch, I thought. I could see two posts down the way a bit, one of them a light post and the other some kind of road sign. I thought, *If I try to get back onto the road before we come to those posts, I'll run the risk of wiping out on this loose gravel. I'll tap on the brake, steer between the posts, and then turn onto the road.* I proceeded to do just that.

When we had skinned our way between the posts (which John says were hardly wide enough to permit our passage) and had regained the road, I stopped tapping on the "brake" and found the car returning to the fifty-five miles per hour still registered on the cruise control. I had been tapping on the accelerator!

John looked at me and said quietly, "That was a humbling experience, wasn't it?"

As we continued on our trip, words began to rise from within me as from a deep bubbling fountain: "He loves me—God loves me—He really loves me!" I had always known that in my mind and, to some degree, with my heart. But this new *knowing* included the brand-new dimension of assurance that God is on the *throne* of my life. I had been asleep at the wheel, out of control, and He was alert on my behalf, defending, guiding, and delivering me from the results of my own error! To this day we cannot understand what kept the car from plummeting straight into the rocky hillside. Somehow it turned itself, or it was turned by God. The greatest miracle of deliverance had happened in midair while I was still asleep!

When we arrived home after the weekend conference, a phone call came from a friend, Marian Stilkey.

"What were you doing last Thursday about ten o'clock in the morning? I was typing, and suddenly the Lord called me to pray for you. And I did—fervently—for about ten or fifteen minutes!" That was the exact time of our trip through the gravel ditch. I *knew* that not only is the Lord aware of my predicaments—He is also able to call others across space to pray for me when I'm totally helpless.

From that day on, my "weekend God" has become more and more an ever-present, live-in Father who is there, no more than a breath away.

> O Lord, Thou hast searched me and known me.
> Thou dost know when I sit down and when I rise up;
> Thou dost understand my thought from afar.
> Thou dost scrutinize my path and my lying down,
> And art intimately acquainted with all my ways....
>
> Where can I go from Thy Spirit?
> Or where can I flee from Thy presence?...
>
> If I take the wings of the dawn,
> If I dwell in the remotest part of the sea,
> Even there Thy hand will lead me,
> And Thy right hand will lay hold of me.
>
> —PSALM 139:1–10

Before this I had had an unbelieving heart; I could not believe God would be there for *me*, though I had taught His faithfulness to others across the country!

⊰II⊱

I (John) had a gentle, kind father who was also a traveling salesman gone much of the time. During the summer of 1979 I found myself puzzling over why thoughts of unbelief so often trooped through my mind. In airports or while driving on busy freeways, I would find myself thinking, *How can God really be concerned about every detail of all these people's lives?* Or, *How can He actually know every hair that falls from every one of these teeming millions of heads?* (Matt. 10:30; Luke 12:7). My mind insisted, "This is purely a logical matter. After all, that's a reasonable question to ask." But my spirit was not at rest. I knew something else was involved.

Finally I thought to ask the Lord, whose reply was instant: "Your father had little time to notice what you were doing." That revealed my inner world of judgments! I had judged, "Dad wouldn't see, compliment, affirm, or care." Never mind that he did, in fact, do those things when he was home. My bitter root grew because he wasn't always there. So, of course, God wouldn't be there for me. And I worked so hard for Him! Then I saw that those thoughts plagued my mind most especially whenever Paula and I were busy serving the Lord. The little boy had been hurt because he worked so hard and received so little notice for it, and the grown one subconsciously expected God to treat him like that, too.

It wasn't noble or very self-flattering to admit to that kind of peevish anger, so the place where that steam happened to vent was in pesky wonderings disguised as cool, clear logic. The heart could not believe. God would be too busy elsewhere to be there for me.

Following the revelation, repentance was easy and joyous. The result has been that I have never since been bothered by such nagging doubts. Now I do not merely have belief, but *surety* of knowing and feeling that my Father sees and approves of my service to Him. Now I have abiding, rather than occasional, fellowship with Him, in heart as well as spirit (1 John 1:3).

How many of us have come to our parents for something, and they said, "We'll see," and then forgot about it? Or we pleaded with Dad to come home early and take us to the movies or ball game or something, and he promised—but didn't come? Or our parents made a promise to buy us something (a bike, fishing equipment, new coat), and we waited and waited. But either it never arrived or came so late the joy of it was gone. Covertly, that colored our faith in God. What kind of anger did we push down and forget, because, "It's not good to be angry with Dad and Mom!" What kind of resentful judgments did our hearts cherish and our minds forget?

GOD'S MERCIFUL ANSWER

In February 1979 the Lord had been teaching Paula and me about Psalm 62:5: "My soul, wait thou only upon God; for my expectation is from him" (KJV). And, "He will give you the desires of your heart" (Ps. 37:4). He had been showing us that the word *wait* is not primarily a reference to time, as we had thought, but speaks of a quality of faith. Unknown to us, "wait" hooks into bitter disappointment about absent fathers and to the childish agonies of waiting hour after hour for some hoped-for moment that sometimes never arrives at all.

On February 14 snow lay two feet deep. That evening Paula and I and Janet Wilcox (who was then visiting us) decided to take a walk around the block. For the first time I noticed how the neighbors' driveways and sidewalks looked. Snowblowers had done neat, effective work. We were still in the "make-do" mentality of our upbringing in depression days—a coal shovel would do fine. But we often ran out of time and energy and had a huge area to clear. I thought, *Lord, I ought to have a snowblower, but those things cost a small fortune. Well, forget it. I can't afford one. Praise You, Lord, anyway.* That was my "faithful, fervent, and earnest" prayer (James 5:16). We said nothing else to anyone. At the time, a man who had flown in from Colorado for prayer ministry was in town. The next day an appliance dealer delivered a five-horsepower snowblower—a gift from the man from Colorado! The Lord was beginning to reach another area of our unbelieving hearts.

That same evening we were packing to speak in a city in Montana. I thought, *Styles have changed. I ought to have a vested suit. My two old suits are both blue. I need a brown vested suit. Well, those cost money, and I don't have any. Forget that. Thank You, Lord, anyway.* The next evening after our first talk, a man introduced himself and said, "I own the local clothing store. One way I pay my tithe is to outfit the Lord's servants who come to speak in our town. Come on down in the morning—better yet, I'll pick you up, and we'll see what we can do." The next morning he walked up to a rack and pulled out an expensive, gold-colored jacket. It was a good fit. He said, "It's yours." Then he grabbed a very expensive brown vested suit that also fit me perfectly. (I hadn't mentioned a word of what I needed.) "What else do you need, John?"

I spluttered and finally blurted out, "Some shorts. I need some shorts." He handed me six pairs of shorts, six undershirts, ten pairs of socks, two pairs of shoes, two pairs of sports pants to go with the jacket, two dress shirts, two sport shirts, and two ties! Humbled and grateful, I knew the Lord was expansively and delightedly writing on my heart, "It is your Father's *good pleasure* to give you the kingdom" (Luke 12:32, KJV, emphasis added)—and that right away, not after long delays.

My heart had been impure. I couldn't see His faithfulness and had often ruefully called Him "the 11:59 God." How little that sanctified His nature (Num. 20:12). Now Paula and I know, more than just intellectually, that He will supply our need even before we know we have one: "For your Father knows what you need, *before* you ask Him" (Matt. 6:8, emphasis added). He moved, in delightful ways, to convert our unbelieving hearts—and we repented of our judgments on our fathers.

We have all lived with criticism; some have experienced it worse than others. For most of us, it came from our parents, and that hurt deeply. Or it came from brothers, sisters, aunts, grandparents, peers, or teachers. Our responses, whether expressed or repressed, were often angry. Consequently, bitter-root judgments lodged in our hearts. We expected people to criticize us from then on—and dutifully, they usually did. Unbeknownst to us, that also dimmed our view of God. How many of us who have learned to listen to God have imagined we heard Him pointing out our failings after a sincere attempt to serve Him?

I (John) used to think, after presenting some thought or idea to a group, that it was the Lord who was criticizing me for things I had said or done wrong, or things I *ought* to have done but had forgotten. Then one day I heard Tommy Tyson teach on the difference between the Lord's *correction* and Satan's *accusation*! I began to ponder this in my heart. Shortly thereafter the Lord caused James 1:5 to leap off the page at me: "If any of you lack wisdom, let him ask of God, that giveth to all men liberally, *and upbraideth not;* and it shall be given him" (KJV, emphasis added). The Word pierced my heart. That criticizing voice had never belonged to the Holy Spirit! God the Father would have waited until the right moment and then gently and kindly talked it out with me: "Come now, and let us reason together, saith the LORD: though your sins be as scarlet, they shall be as white as snow; though they be red like crimson, they shall be as wool" (Isa. 1:18, KJV). I repented then of my judgments on my parents and God and of my denial of God's nature by believing that Satan's accusations were God's. I could not see God's gentle, affirming nature. My heart had remained unconverted in that stony area due to my unconfessed sin. Praise God for His holy and gentle conviction! I have never again felt attacked or criticized by the Lord. He only affirms and comforts—and later sits down to reason, considerately calling me to account, and I like it.

Perhaps the most important way we all fail to see God is in the most basic—love. Few of us had parents who could, and did, take the initiative to regularly comfort and give affection when we needed it. Some had parents who hugged and kissed only in front of company or when they felt expansive, but not at times that were appropriate to the signals we gave. We learned to detest that kind of offer; it exploited us instead of blessed us. Most of the people I have ministered to insist that their parents did not initiate action appropriate to their needs in childhood, and many complain that their parents never showed affection at all. So we learned to define love not as a sacrificial, steadfast, daily giving, with sensitivity to what others want, but as some kind of vague sense of being half-wanted, when someone feels like touching us. That clouded our heart's picture of God, no matter what our minds learned to think of Him.

The entire Bible is the history of God taking the initiative to come to deliver all mankind and us personally. We see that basic fact, if we have eyes at all to read. But in the daily practice of devotional life, we strive to reach a God who we actually think in our hearts may not be listening after all. We feel alone (when we never could be). We don't expect God to be sending His angels to rescue and His servants to heal before we cry out. Never mind the Scriptures about His leaving the ninety-nine in the fold (Luke 15:4–7): "He wouldn't come after me unless I do something first or deserve it." Our dirty hearts see God clothed in our parents' mannerisms. In such areas we are unconverted in heart.

In his classic work *Faust,* Goethe wrote of history: "'Tis thus at the roaring Loom of Time I ply, and weave for God the Garment thou seest Him by." How fantastically true! All mankind's history teaches us at our heart's level that God is created in our image instead of the other way around. Our own personal history, every moment of it, is a fabric by which we see God. All our judgments become colored glasses that darken the face of God. No wonder He says, "'For my thoughts are not your thoughts, neither are your ways My ways,' declares the LORD. 'For as the heavens are higher than the earth, so are My ways higher than your ways, and My thoughts than your thoughts'" (Isa. 55:8–9).

From the moment of our first conversion, the Holy Spirit is given license to work upon our hearts, to reveal and convict. The Christian life of sanctification and transformation is therefore:

> Beloved, now we are children of God, and it has not appeared as yet what we shall be. We know that, when He appears, we shall be like Him, because we shall see Him just as He is. And *everyone who has this hope fixed on Him purifies himself,* just as He is pure.
>
> —1 JOHN 3:2–3, EMPHASIS ADDED

OPENING BLINDED EYES

Christian pastors, counselors, and lay leaders are meant to be God's sharpest tools for that purification and transformation process to be effected in every believer's life. Just as God has raised some priests to be ordained among the priesthood of all believers, and some prophets to be recognized as such, though we all are, so too He has raised up prayer ministers and lay leaders who are especially gifted to perceive the practices of the flesh.

However, this work of taking captive areas of the imagination (2 Cor. 10:4–5) is the work of every brother and sister for every other brother and sister. How many countless ways do our forgotten judgments prevent us from seeing the true life of God manifested among us? When a child is faced with parental adulteries, carousings and lies, fear of hearing loud voices in the night, and violence in his parents' lives, what picture of God does that child develop?

Consider how the inability of a father or mother to sympathize or understand portrays God's nature to the heart: "God wouldn't or couldn't understand me."

Or how does God appear to a child who is always controlled and told that what he thinks is not really what he thinks, or that his talent is worthless? If he judges his parents, there is no way that child could feel free to assert who and what he is, or expect that God would be delighted in him and would cherish him for his own talents. So it goes, in myriads of inner darknesses.

After many years of ministering to others, Paula and I are still discovering, as we have related here, more and more areas in which our own forgotten but still active childhood judgments of our parents have blinded our eyes to God. And we had good, loving, well-intentioned parents. What of the many who have been so fiercely wounded? St. Paul said, "I press on to know Him" (Phil. 3:12).

Our first conversion has resurrected our inner Lazarus. Now let us be members of that fellowship of Bethany called by Christ to take the grave clothes off one another's hands, feet, and faces (John 11:44) so we may behold life and walk with Him and hold His hand.

Perhaps the following poem, written by a Holy Spirit–filled friend in a moment of inspiration in a Christian camp, expresses better than all in prose:

> I'm not the same on the outside
> as I am on the inside.
> I smile, I laugh.
> But I don't know joy.
> Where is my joy, O my God?
> Why have You forsaken me?
> Everything was once so free…
> Once grass was green,
> and hills were pretty.
> Now I seem to see them through

a veil of gray.
Inside is cold and tight and sad.
I cry and ache. Most days
I long for eyes to see me.
But I hide so well, none can see.
I know it's me, but then I think,
They don't care—*He* must not care.

But too long I have known His love,
And I know this is not true.
Yet, I am unable to get above,
and I am sinking slowly in the sands.
"Help," I say—inside I scream—
but on my face, I smile.
Only my eyes express—the well
of pain in me.
I'm careful not to look at those
who might strip away my mask.
But I want it to come down, at last
Reality to grasp.
I cannot do this for myself.
Am I ready for You at last?

"Honesty," we cry,
"transparency," and the like.
But who will brave this scary turf?
I've been brave, I've tried.
But from openness came pain, from
those who want to close my door,
who trample my little girl.
So light and gay is she, but oh, so sensitive,
and too many times others have driven
her in.
"Come out, little girl," I coax,
but she just sits and mopes,
No longer can I coax her out.

Are you sleeping, little girl?
Lord, send someone to love her to
life, once more.

—Anonymous

Amen to that prayer. Lord, send laborers into the harvest. Send prayer ministers and lay leaders to the blind in heart.

CHAPTER 3

PERFORMANCE ORIENTATION

You foolish Galatians! Who has bewitched you? Before your very eyes Jesus Christ was clearly portrayed as crucified. I would like to learn just one thing from you: Did you receive the Spirit by observing the law, or by believing what you heard? Are you so foolish? After beginning with the Spirit, are you now trying to attain your goal by human effort?

—GALATIANS 3:1–3, NIV

THE CONSTANT PROPENSITY OF the born anew is to fall back to striving by human effort. Our minds and spirits know the free gift of salvation, but our hearts retain their habit to earn love by performing. Most commonly, we who are "saved" are unaware ("bewitched") that other motives than God's love have begun to corrupt us into striving, tension, and fear; or, suspecting, we fail to know which, why, or what wrong motive.

Performance orientation is a term that refers not to the service we perform but to the false motives that impel us. Having brought performance orientation to death, we may do exactly the same works, in much the same ways, but from an entirely different intent in the heart. In bringing performance to death we are not saying to stop serving and doing, but to die to the wrong hidden motives in the heart.

As little children we all in some degree accept lies and build them into our nature. The most pervasive, destructive lie corroding all our actions is, "If I don't do right, I won't be loved." "If I can't be like Mommy and Daddy want, I won't belong." Sometimes even the conscious mind believes that error; more commonly it lodges like a snake hidden in the grass, slithering through all our efforts. Unseen, unknown enemies have far more cogency than the known. For the performance-oriented, the base of all life is not restful acceptance and consequent confidence, but constant anxiety, fear, and striving.

The lie becomes part of us through common daily acts in our childhood, such as potty training. "Oh, you did good. Mommy loves you." Of course, Mommy would have loved us no matter how many times we messed our pants, but in our childish minds we connected performing with love and soon arrived at the inverse, "If I don't do right (on the potty or anywhere else), Mommy won't love me." Performing may soon so intertwine falsely with love that we cannot conceive of being loved unless we have performed rightly. Or worse, we come to believe that not performing earns rejection, so even if someone gives us love, we think we didn't deserve it. As a result, either we won't receive love offered, or false guilt assails.

Mothers normally don't intend to teach wrong things. It just happens, again and again. "Oh, you look great in your new dress; Mommy loves you." The child may take home the message that good appearances earn love (and sloppiness or ugliness lose it). "You slept *all* night and didn't cry once. I'm proud of you, son; I love you." Right away we may slip the hand of love into the prickly glove of striving to please. So simply and easily our hearts laminate what ought to be separated—behaving well and being loved. We learn to fish for love, every action a lure. No action, no fish (equals no love), and to our minds deservedly so. It all becomes a delusion.

Now let us add the many mistaken forms of correction most of us have endured. We hear: "Where did my little boy go? He was here a moment ago. This can't be my little boy who acts like this." Thus we are directly told that what we actually are is unacceptable. Our identity must become the doll image, the picture someone else has created for us to act out. Fear of failing to be that identity strikes at the heart. We dread becoming lost from ourselves and from others, and so we lock ourselves into performing. Ironically, to the degree that we succeed in acting out what is wanted, we do in fact become lost from what would have been us.

ALLOWED TO BE ME?

Children need to misbehave sometimes. That's what children are: rascals with angelic eyes and dirty skin. "Foolishness is bound up in the heart of a child; the rod of discipline will remove it far from him" (Prov. 22:15). A child's foolishness needs to be checked by firm hands and each child given parameters while being warmly held and accepted—especially when acting at his worst. That says love is unconditional. It writes into the heart that love is a gift fully given and never lost. Love creates security.

But many parents use a child's need for love to try to control— "I can't love you when you act like that." How dreadfully damaging to a child! "Help! I must remember what I am supposed to be! What if I can't... or won't do it? Oh, nobody can love me. I don't deserve it." If he could voice it, the child would say, "I'm angry. Why can't they just love me as I am?" So, out of dread, he sets himself to earn love.

"Now go to your room, and when you can act like you, you can come out again." The translation of such a communication is: "Only the performer is acceptable here. If you don't perform up to our standards, you earn rejection."

"Leave the table! When you can come out wearing a smile, you can be part of the family again. We're not going to have an old grump around here." Real message: "Love is not unconditional around here. You are not free to express honestly. Lie, and put on a hypocritical face. Then we can accept you." Our spirit knows better than that, but fear and the need to belong master us, so we make ourselves act out what we are not.

Not only is a child told in many ways that letting the real one live earns rejection, but also parents may add to the message by intimating that the real one ought not to exist at all. From then on, honest impulses of anger, frivolity, or spontaneity are identified as "not us," something to be suppressed or avoided. At last the inner being quits trying and dies, and the hollow shell performs, devoid of real abundant life. Until that kind of wrongful death, the inner being keeps trying to live. As a result, duality of personality is basic to all of us.

I grew up with the message, "A Sandford man never hits a girl." That was a fine teaching that to this day I am grateful for and still live by. But what was I to do with the part of me that wanted to wallop my sister, Martha Jane? To have to learn to check my feelings and make appropriate choices was good. But on what basis did I make such choices? Was it from love in my heart and respect for my father and mother and brothers and sister, or was it because I was afraid I wouldn't be a Sandford? Perhaps a mixture of both? Was fear not to belong more the ruling factor than love? Which motive actually governed me? Which motive still governs me today?

A simple rule is this: where much laughter and affection are present, children learn they are accepted no matter how well or poorly they perform. They are free to be. When children who have just goofed badly can leap into their parents' arms, and all can laugh and learn (even if discipline has to be applied), children learn that the nasty side is also me and is loved and lovable, too. "Love covers a multitude of sins" (1 Pet. 4:8). Nowhere is that more true than in the helter-skelter of children's emotions. Unconditional love, not taken for granted, but often expressed, grants security to venture all sides of the "me" a child is discovering, and freedom to choose which modes to settle into, from an altogether different base than fear.

Conversely, uptight, rigid demands of behavior without affection clamp upon children manacles of control: "You will not be loved unless you can deserve it." Once that lie is grafted in, it becomes the governing trunk to all our fruit. All our actions flow through that stem.

Even in the warmest, most secure families, anxiety normally tinges freedom with fear. An infant can play peek-a-boo for hours and giggle every time Daddy or Mommy comes out from behind the covering. Children, perhaps from birth trauma into a sinful world, have great inner fear of being left or rejected. The game of peek-a-boo acts out that fear and gives assurance again and again—because each time Mommy and Daddy are still there. Even in warm, loving families, we can fear blowing the good life, fear dishonoring the family, fear that, after all, we might be unacceptable if we prove to be too different from everybody else.

Therefore, the rule is: *anxiety is augmented to dread and compliant performance to the degree of coldness and rigidity in the family behavioral pattern.* To that degree, fear binds all life: "who through fear of death were subject to slavery all their lives" (Heb. 2:15). The death we fear is not physical death. To the performance-oriented believer, physical death would mean release. Rather, we fear dying to that world of control we have falsely come to believe guarantees us belonging and love. That fear of death prevents even the born anew from change—until love reaches frozen corners and death of self sets us free.

CHARACTERISTICS OF
PERFORMANCE ORIENTATION

Performance orientation does not define one who works hard, but one who works hard for the wrong reasons. A free person may work harder in the same works—impelled only by love. Performance-oriented people require constant affirmation (unconsciously demanding it, sometimes verbally). They cannot handle criticism well. Their security is not first in God and themselves but in what people think of them. They are dependent upon the reactions of others. They have little center of decision in themselves. They must become whatever it takes to gain approval from others.

They have become what Erich Fromm calls "market-oriented personalities" who sell themselves to be or do whatever purchases for them signs of acceptance.[1] Reproofs are taken defensively, not as signs of acceptance and love, but as rejection. Guilt cannot easily be admitted because that is translated into, "I didn't try," "I don't belong," and "I must keep trying to belong or I am lost." Give a rebuke to a performance-oriented person, and you may be astonished to hear, "You're telling me I don't love you." Secure persons living with performance-oriented people often marvel, "How did he/she get that out of what I said?" Emotional outbursts can erupt from the smallest or even unintended slights, and we are amazed to hear, "How could you ever doubt that I love you?" usually followed by, "After all I've *done* for you," or, "You don't appreciate me. You never do."

Performance-oriented people dole out affection by measure according to how well the primary people around them have behaved. Love is not given when others haven't done well: "They don't deserve it." Having been dealt with that way, they do it to others. How many husbands have been chagrined to discover that their wives' ability to cherish them sexually is connected to how well they themselves have behaved—according to *her* standards? Sex becomes a weapon of control. Or how often do we give each other the cold shoulder or the silent treatment, intending by that to control the other, to drive him to do what we want?

Christian love ought to be opposite to performance-oriented behavior. The Word-become-flesh is love given unconditionally, unvaried by the good or bad behavior of the other. Christian love is born in the unfailing heart of Christ in us for the other. How we act out that love may vary according to the other's behavior, to be appropriate to the needs of the moment. Rebuke may be the action love requires. Or tenderness. Or withdrawal. We are governed not by insecurity but by the flow of Christ's love in wisdom. Unfortunately, however, we have developed sinful structures in a pre-Christian life. Performance orientation has been built in. It is the warp and woof of us. The Holy Spirit must find ways to pour love out from the center of that tangled bramble bush we have become—and many people get stuck on the not-yet-dead thorny points of us. We still use love to control until death of self proceeds to deliverance.

Performance-oriented people are sometimes afraid to try new things. It isn't OK to fail. Not that they don't sometimes try new things. Performance orientation may drive them to venture wildly, or it may cause them to be strong enough to prevent innate creature drives. But the point is fear. All normal people fear, but in performance-oriented people, fear of failure rises more out of what loved ones and others will think of them than how failure may hurt another. Security that makes fun of trial and error is gone. The performance-oriented person wants to know what the rules are beforehand. The subliminal messages are: "Tell me how to do it so I can feel secure." "I want to know before I venture so I can feel good about myself." "I need to be in control." Therefore, performance-oriented people cannot be spontaneous—unless they can playact it as a part of doing what are the roles of the party. Self-control is a virtue for them to the point of idolatry and rigidity. They are always poised and correct—in public.

Sometimes the burden becomes too heavy. The more people and new circumstances such a person encounters, the more subliminally he must work to find out the rules and roles. Thrown under too much pressure, he may crack up or fall into depression. He cannot conceive that he is accepted just because he exists, but only if he conforms to prevailing patterns.

If a performance-oriented person belongs to groups whose mores conflict with his own, shifting gears nearly tears him apart. For example, the husband who works for a demanding, obscene, burly, macho boss then comes home to live with a demure, righteous Christian wife. He finds that all day he must act tough, speak obscenely, and share dirty jokes, only to come home and act like a saint. Putting the two together at the annual Christmas party spells torture. The burden of trying to find out and act in whatever way buys the love he needs may become so heavy that he will flip out in fright or rebellion—drunken sprees, being spaced out on drugs, gambling, having an affair, or whatever blows the role of the good guy or vents the hidden anger that comes from having to perform.

Since performance-oriented people have little center of their own and must act out whatever the group model is, this goes far to explain why so many "good" boys seem to have so little resistance to doing wrong when in bad company. They were never that moral from a base of love, but only by virtue of performing according to their parents' standards. Present temptations laminate two powerful drives: one, to break out of the mold and do something to blow the whole role, and two, to belong to the gang that presents the temptation.

RESULTS OF PERFORMANCE ORIENTATION

Performance-oriented people may lose their true identities. A child faces choices, hundreds of times a week, whether to act out the doll image the parents require or to express his real feelings. A person developing performance orientation must repress the actual again and again. Several things begin to result:

1. The inner being finally gives up sending messages until the person feels he is what he is acting out.

2. Below the level of consciousness, the performance-oriented person feels prostituted. He resents having to sell himself for the reward "money" of love.

3. Mounting anger causes him to develop a "loser"—a need to lose. He wants to do something drastic enough to destroy the whole spurious game. He wants no longer simply to have to believe that he is loved. He wants to discover as fact, expressed and experienced, that he is still loved if he does everything wrong and becomes what is to him totally unlovable.

4. Therefore, he becomes a powder keg, looking for a match to give him an excuse to blow up.

Many times Paula and I have ministered to people who have become successes in their chosen fields, only to "explode" and lose it all. Precisely at the moment when they could have enjoyed rest (Heb. 4:9–11), they themselves blow the whole thing. They fall into alcoholism, gamble, have an affair, or develop some excruciating obvious psychosomatic illness—anything to lose! They can't understand why. It's all a mystery to them, and unfair!

There are some simple reasons. First, during all their striving to succeed, their inner being had to be told, "Lie down; we have work to do." Normal interior needs for alternation, rest, expression of anger, wild impulses, fantasies, and so forth had to be sacrificed to the outer drive to succeed, or so it seemed. That is like holding a ball under water. The moment exterior demands slacken, inner drives shoot up, exploding great splashes in every direction. Like an impatient child throwing a temper tantrum, the inner self screams through the losing circumstances for its chance to be heard.

Second, during all the striving, the outer man tells the inner, "When we get there (million dollars, stardom, acclaim, whatever), then we'll be able to rest." Arrival threatens to reveal delusion—the person feels no more approved of, loved, or secure. Success was the wrong answer for the wrong question. Another million, another pinnacle has to be achieved, else we have to admit the whole game was hollow—but we can't do that because performing has been our entire definition of what it is to have life and be loved! The alternative *seems* to be laziness or, worse, rejection, and emptiness of all purpose in life. Money and success were never actually the performance-oriented person's goals, even if he thought they were. The goal was the power to feel good and acceptable—to himself and others. So the Marilyn Monroes commit suicide, and the Morgans go on to try to own the whole world.

One Midwestern pastor was raised by a mother who never gave affection and demanded behavior. He felt the pressure of performing so keenly that he projected his own inner demand, created mainly by his reactions to his mother, onto his wife. He just couldn't live with that woman another minute. She made life a prison house for him (he thought), demanding that he live up to her expectations. She came for prayer ministry and changed. It made no difference whatsoever; to him she was the problem. (If he could have located his anger at his mother, he could have stopped projecting, but he had her too well protected from himself—after all, it's not nice to hate mommies.)

This pastor was an evangelical, born-again preacher. Saving souls was his business, and he was good at it. But his own heart had not yet heard what he preached. He was no hypocrite; he was merely a man caught in not-yet-dead flesh. He felt prostituted, by and for his wife and the whole church. He had a desperate need to do something drastic enough to escape the treadmill. I (John) saw this and warned him, "You have a hidden hatred for your mother. You need to defile a woman. If you don't deal with this, you are going to do something drastic."

"Oh, no, John," he replied. "I'm saved. Christ died for all that in me. I've claimed it. That's all dead. How could a born-again, Holy Spirit–filled man have all that in him?" The problem was "out there." If I couldn't help him "shape up his wife," he would have no further part of any prayer ministry with me.

The man was unaware of his own motives, therefore the inevitable adulterous affair was not only purposefully not hidden, but it was also especially crude and carnal—further, he *had* to blab about it. Why? To make sure the entire good-guy image was sufficiently destroyed. Fortunately, the wife and the elders to whom he blabbed forgave, received, cherished, and sent him back to me for "rehabilitation"; today he is still the pastor of that church and is on his way to wholeness! (Confession to elders is good; his original confession was not confession, however, but childish self-tattling.)

One of our dear friends, raised as an only child, born late to cold and distant parents, had no awareness at all of love without earning it. He would perform well, but every so often would go on a drinking spree. After one such spree, in a rare moment of truth, he told his wife, "I'm going to test you again and again until I know for sure you really love me." Sure enough, he did, again and again, including not-too-hidden adulteries. She forgave at increasing cost, persistently. Love had to be given unconditionally until she found she no longer could give love, and in despair, she discovered that only Jesus in her could give this kind of love. At last his heart believed, and he turned around.

The Danger of Shrikism

At what seems to me (John) the worst level, performance orientation can produce *shrikes*. A *shrike* is a bird that tears its victims apart muscle by muscle. In humans, a shrike is a person who so gathers all the righteousness to herself/himself (more commonly a woman) that the other (usually the mate, often the husband) has no room to express righteousness and acts out the role of the villain. In these persons, performance orientation is usually combined with sibling rivalry (the child learned to ace out the other siblings by out-performing for whatever scraps of parental praise were available), coupled with bitter-root expectancy that others will fail to serve as well or do right at all. Bitter-root expectancy in a shrike broadcasts to the mate twenty-four hours a day: "Do wrong. Do me in. I know you will. Make me into a noble martyr. That's the way I expect life to go. That's the role I play (without admitting it). That's the role I want you to play."

One lady came to me (John) wanting to know why her husband was such a weakling, falling again and again into drunken binges. She was a paragon of virtue—in dress, morals, posture, church attendance, and prayer life. You name it, she was it, the "saintess" of the church. Beneath all her behavior was not pure love for others but a self-serving need to be perfect, coupled with bitter-root expectancy that the man (her father had been a drunkard) would be weak. I sat and watched as they entered into a spat. Everything but her actual words screamed at her husband her demand that he be the weakling she needed. Understandably, the more secure he became and the less he drank, the more upset rather than glad she became. Her whipping post was deserting her. Her ability to feel good about herself depended upon being able to contrast his failure against her own supposed virtue. This made her the perpetual noble martyr, supported in all those feelings by her Job's comforters in the church: "Isn't she a wonderful Christian living with that awful man?" Tragically, she is far from an isolated case; the pattern is almost endemic.

Shrikism happens in women more than men, not because men are better (they aren't), but because women are built by God to want to please more than men. They fall more naturally into performance orientation than men do. Lacking physical power, women learn as girls to use emotional wiles and, forgetting that, may unconsciously use performance to ace out the husband and play the noble martyr. Men with other men tend to rebellion more often than to compliance, but having been raised with controlling mothers, they are more susceptible to performance for a wife, though less apt to be shrikes.

RELIGION OR FAITH?

In the church, performance orientation becomes a religious spirit rather than Christian. *Religion* is defined (in my big Oxford Dictionary) as "action or conduct indicating a belief in, reverence for, and a *desire to please* a divine ruling power" (emphasis added). Theologically, religion is defined as man's search for God, man using Bible study, church attendance, good works, and devotion to try to find and *please* God.

Christian faith is the opposite. It is God finding man, giving to mankind out of His unfailing heart of love. In religion, man hangs on to God. In faith, God hangs on to man. In religion, there is striving, fear, and false guilt—we're never good enough; we can never quite make it. In faith, there is rest and peace, because the enterprise of us has been released into the Father's hands, and He will do a better job with us than we can. In faith, all striving (Col. 2:1; 1 Tim. 4:10; Heb. 4:11; 12:4) is undergirded with peace. God has us. We are loved and chosen. We may fall out of fellowship temporarily, but not out of love, and when we do, He will come and get us. So we are secure. We are free to goof, and because we are, we need to less often.

Religious people have transferred performance orientation to God. Now they most emphatically have a Father whose "demands" *have* to be lived up to! Never mind that God the Father isn't at all like that. He wears the overlay of our life with our earthly parents.

(See chapter two, "Seeing God With an Unbelieving Heart.") Therefore, as soon as the original relief of redemption passes and the Holy Spirit comes, performance-oriented people think in their hearts, below the level of conscious thought, *Now I really ought to be able to live up to it!* and set themselves to strive to be perfect, not actually for the love of Jesus, but out of the same old carnal fear of parental rejection. Unfortunately, all too many sermons scold and exhort for performance, building the same fearful striving instead of preaching the simple good news of God's grace to little children peering out of adult eyes.

Religious people (POs* born anew) become centers of dissension in the church. They criticize others and cannot receive rebuke in return. It was the religious leaders who crucified Jesus, and religious leaders have persecuted the faithful every since. Religious people are the Pharisees of today.

> And the Pharisees and some of the scribes gathered together around Him when they had come from Jerusalem, and had seen that some of His disciples were eating their bread with impure hands, that is, unwashed. (For the Pharisees and all the Jews do not eat unless they carefully wash their hands, thus observing the traditions of the elders; and when they come from the market place, they do not eat unless they cleanse themselves; and there are many other things which they have received in order to observe, such as the washing of cups and pitchers and copper pots.)
>
> —MARK 7:1–4

Their security depended upon doing the "right" things—ritual washings and ceremonial rites—not on knowing His love for them or in doing acts of love. Jesus upset their world. They had carefully

---

* An abbreviation that will be used in place of the term "performance orientation" or "performance oriented."

built that system of proper behaviors to insure righteousness for themselves and to ace out all the siblings who failed to perform as well as they. (The same is often true in the church today.) Along came Jesus, and by His love and merciful flaunting of their Sabbath laws, He told them that all their work-righteousness was to no avail. In no way could they feel His love—apart from rites and rituals. The alternative seemed emptiness. He was a menace. He undid them. Therefore they hated Him—and they still do today, even though they are born anew and naming His name in worship every Sunday in His church!

CHRIST IS THE KEY

The great tragedy is not that PO people persecute those of restful faith, but that the faithful have not known how to minister to them to set them free. Believers must learn how to love strivers to rest. Nowhere else in all society can a PO person find rest, for only after he has again and again tested love offered can he settle it in his heart that he is OK just because he exists in Christ. The world will not so continue to accept and forgive. *In Christ* is the key, for any man's spirit will be open to the accusation of Satan until he knows in the depths of his heart that, imperfect as he is, he is OK just as he is because the Lord Jesus Christ has become his strength, his salvation, and his song.

Satan seeks a prey whom he *can* devour (1 Pet. 5:8)! Paradoxically, the one he *can* devour is the one who thinks he must have some righteousness or be undone. In whatever area and to whatever degree a man has accepted the PO lie that he must do right in order to be loved, Satan has a playing field. He can always come along and point out some area of failure. The one he cannot touch is the one who knows he remains a sinner, though redeemed, without any righteousness of his own, needing none, because Jesus is his righteousness.

Behavior still needs to be in accordance with the standards set by our Lord Jesus Christ. Being without righteousness does not mean freedom as a pretext for evil (Gal. 5:13). Behavior will follow as an outcome of His love in us. But success or failure in behavior is not the mark of our righteousness—Jesus is.

You do not escape performance orientation or a religious spirit by leaving the church, nor by abandoning moral laws, which may seem to the PO person to be a prison. The structure of PO is internal; we take it wherever we go, like the old saying, "You can take the boy out of the farm, but then you have to take the farm out of the boy." Wherever one is in society, performance is demanded.

Nowhere is performance more fearsomely controlled by peers than in criminal society! Criminal societies admit people in or cancel people out solely according to how well they perform. In my Yellow Cab driver days, I (John) used to answer the dispatcher and find myself transporting girls to "work." (By law a taxi driver must take passengers where they want to go.) I was continually surprised listening to these prostitutes complaining bitterly about other girls who "didn't do it right." They "give our whole profession a bad name"—as though it didn't have one already! Businesses, clubs, friends, even chance acquaintanceships all contain imperious demands for behavior and penalties for noncompliance. The only *emotional* difference outside or inside the church is that in the church the Lord Jesus Christ has a chance to bring us to death and consequent rest in the relaxing grace of God.

Obstinacy in the Heart

The internal structure of performance orientation forms a most obstinate area of unbelief in the heart among born-anew Christians. The mind hears the message of the free gift, and the spirit sighs in relief, but the heart has long been trained to strive to please for wrong reasons. As said earlier, soon after the glow of conversion dies down, performance resurrects with a vengeance, and now the Christian in dead earnest has a Father and demanding standards to live up to! Many come into the fullness of the Holy Spirit only to crack up subsequently because that undead area of the flesh throws them into an inner striving no one can live up to! An individual who has learned PO from her father now has a heavenly Father whom she strives to please. The flesh grandly transfers onto the Father God all her striving to earn her natural father's love and heaps the whole weight of Christ's example on her. Life quickly becomes impossible. She often slumps into depression.

It is not that we should give up trying to live for Christ. What needs to happen is death of old motives and birth of the new. Before we are crucified, behind all our serving is the striving of the flesh. We obey law in whatever degree we are able to do so to win brownie points, for fear of punishment, to earn the Father's love, out of duty because we were trained to, for fear we can't live with our false and accusing conscience, for threat of what others will think of us or that we won't belong—all wrong motives for a Christian. *All of that needs to die.* What should impel us, singly and purely, is the flow of Jesus' love through us. What we do doesn't earn us anything, put anyone in our debt to respond in kind, ensure that we will belong or be loved, or stave off fear. Those things have all been answered by the only true answer—the gift of Jesus. But until our *unbelieving heart* comes *in truth* to apprehend that fact, we will keep on keeping on. We may, having finally died to performance, return to do exactly the same works for the Lord in identical words and ways, but what flows through us will now be Jesus' love, not our flesh, and others will quickly read and take note.

In one church we visited there was a deacon who was "Mr. Everything." He took up the collections each Sunday, sang in the choir, sold the most tickets for the men's banquets, drove shut-ins to church, and volunteered for every job that came along. But he was also "Mr. Thorn-in-the-Side" for the pastor and "Mr. Dissension" in the church. On his face and in his walk was a little boy saying, "Don't you see I'm doing it right? I'm being a good boy. Now you have to love me." In his voice, raised often, was condemnation and criticism. He just couldn't see why "others can't serve the Lord like I do." No way could he hear what was infecting all his serving. He had no awareness of his inner motives. He could not see that his criticisms were not born of love for the Lord but from his child's need to outperform sibling rivals. Since his full-flowered PO could not take the slightest rebuke, he could never hear the kindest explanations of what actually was happening. He has since left the church, thoroughly disappointed with those "backsliders." The church has since become warm, unified, and loving. This deacon was a born-again man on fire for the Lord. What a tragedy and a repentance for us all that we have not understood ministry to the heart, to be the kind of body that could have saved him—an unbelieving believer.

Peggy came to us because her husband had left and she couldn't understand why. She had "done everything for him." Listening to her, I (John) couldn't see what was the real reason for the separation. Then it happened that Peggy was the guest host for a house meeting at which I spoke. The moment I entered, Peggy busied herself, blustering here and there, overserving. On her face and in her manner, even in her walk, she was saying, "I'm performing well for you. Tell me that I am. Don't you feel guilty if you don't?" I knew why her husband left. The poor man could never rest in his own home. With every service she laid a demand on him to respond, to appreciate, to notice. A man gets tired having to prove over and over that he loves and appreciates. She could never simply believe she was loved and rest beside him. She *had* to serve, and he *had* to affirm. "It is better to live in a corner of a roof, than in a house shared with a *contentious woman*" (Prov. 21:9, emphasis added). "It is better to live in a desert land, than with a contentious and *vexing* woman" (Prov. 21:19, emphasis added). "Better is a dry morsel and quietness with it than a house full of feasting with strife" (Prov. 17:1).

I tried to tell her. She too was a born-again, Holy Spirit–filled, believing, churchgoing woman. She knew salvation. But her heart could not receive it and rest. She could not hear me. "An evil man seeketh only rebellion: therefore a cruel messenger shall be sent against him" (Prov. 17:11, KJV). It was not long in coming.

Her husband returned home, but he lost his job. Now he lay on the couch and demanded service. He would not look for a new job; he made her go out and find a job. Not only would he not help straighten up the house or do dishes, but he would not even drive her to work or let her take the car! She had to pedal her bicycle to work, labor all day, pump home, clean up the house and his day's dishes, prepare supper, do dishes, wash clothes, and get ready to do it all over again the next day.

Whenever we continue in our own stubborn way, the kind-though-seeming-unkindness of the Lord is to pile on more and more until we reach the end and become disgusted enough to quit. Finally there came a morning in which, still a half mile from work, Peggy turned to churn against a forty-mile gale! That did it. There on the bike, pumping for all she was worth and getting nowhere, she blew up at God, screaming at the top of her lungs, "Here I am trying to get to work. I'm trying to serve You. I'm loving that no-good husband *You gave me*. I'm doing all that work at home, and he won't help me—and You have to send a storm against me!" That outburst opened the doors and broke her control, and out of Peggy poured all of her pent-up feelings. She cursed, raved, ranted, and wound up shouting obscenities at God! And what happened? No lighting bolts hurtled out of heaven to strike her down. No cars came along to crush and punish. Instead, there came an overwhelming peace. Anointing, blessing, and love poured out of heaven all over her! Right there in the middle of the road she stopped and cried like a baby. For the first time in her life she *knew* someone would love her—even if she didn't do it all right. Her unbelieving heart had finally been evangelized.

A few weeks later, Peggy came to see me, not for prayer ministry but to say "thanks." Always before she had sat on the edge of her chair, knees together, hands folded in the lap, overly prim and proper. Now she lounged comfortably in the deep chair, laughed and joked, and admitted easily and honestly what she actually felt. Incidentally, finding out that it was OK to goof had not caused her to lose her moral nature. (Peggy happens to be one of the most gloriously beautiful blondes a man could wish for.) Now, being moral had become easier, originating from a base of love for God, not from compulsion. She had finally learned the true meaning of grace—undeserved, unmerited favor.

I have to confess that often while ministering to overachievers, in my flesh I have wished they would go out and do something thoroughly prodigal so they could truly learn what it is to have and need a Savior. Martin Luther used to so overconfess to his confessor that finally Spatina shouted at him, "Martin, will you quit wearing me out confessing all these little peccadilloes and go out and do some mighty sin? Then come in here and confess!" Of course, the answer is not to do what Spatina suggested when, in exasperation as a confessor, he exclaimed, "If you must sin, sin mightily!" We don't all, like that pastor mentioned earlier, have to have an affair to discover love and salvation in the heart.

Paula was like that beautiful blonde, thoroughly moral and nearly as performance oriented. In the beginning of our marriage, I could rarely tell her anything that contained rebuke; it would be thrown back on me, with defensive rancor. I had my own faults, much more grievous, but that was one of Paula's. I tried again and again to talk with her about it, but I could never get through to real reception and comprehension. Finally, after sixteen years, I said to the Lord, "I give up. You'll have to get through to her."

At the same time, I (Paula) was saying much the same thing to the Lord: "I give up. I don't know what he's talking about. I don't know how to change. I can't live with this impasse. Do whatever You can,

Lord, to break through." Even at the time as I prayed, I couldn't identify the problems as something in myself. From my point of view I was working hard to fulfill and coordinate efforts in multiple roles: mother of six, high school teacher with preparation to do in four subjects, plus being a minister's wife active in the life of the church. I was striving to succeed in all of this, and John's conversation came as an accusation and burden to suggest that I was not doing enough.

Of course, that was not the message he intended. But that was what I heard. I was exhausted. I wanted him just to love me for me, and I couldn't see that my striving and my defensive walls were preventing him from doing so. Performance-oriented people usually work hard to love by serving others but cannot let others close enough to give them love in return. We have talked to many charismatic Christian leaders since who have become isolated and lonely at the top of the stairs because no one dared to break through their PO to minister to them.

Some friends had spoken to John, "Why can't I get close to Paula?"

He had replied, "I don't know. Ask her." But I carried such poise and control that no one seemed willing or able to tackle me head-on. It seemed that each time I asked for prayer from others, the tough-love words my heart longed to hear never came. Instead it was, "Praise God for this wonderful, strong woman." That missed me totally. I was lonely and angry, and all I knew to do was to try harder. The defensive walls were so thick that if John had been an angel, he would have had difficulty passing through. And he was lonely for me and hurting. "Sometimes I wish I'd married a dumb, talentless blonde," he once said. And I thought, *What an unappreciative nerd.*

God knows that walls too high to leap over and too sturdy to pass through need dismantling. When the two of us finally *gave up*, God ignored even the martyr strain in our cry and answered in a magnificent way.

I was teaching school in Mullan, Idaho, a small town about six miles uphill toward Lookout Pass from Wallace where we lived. It was October, and though the snow had not yet begun to fall, sometimes there were patches of black ice on shaded curves of the road. In the middle of the day I expected the roads to be clear as I drove home in our VW van. Suddenly, at sixty miles per hour, I hit ice (the speed limit was seventy in those days). The weight of the rear engine spun the van like a Tilt-A-Whirl. The van hit the guardrail and rolled two and a half times, and I flew through the front windshield sometime before the van came to rest on its top.

I woke up lying on my back in the middle of the concrete freeway looking into the face of a man I had only met once before. I thought I must be hurt, but I felt no pain and was unbelievably peaceful. Calmly I told the young man to have the ambulance take me to Kellogg Hospital (fourteen miles from the scene of the accident) because that was where our doctor practiced. Inquiring about involvement with any other vehicles, I was assured that there were none, and I felt tremendously relieved. Words of the Twenty-third Psalm ran through my mind over and over all the way to the hospital, but the sense of peace continued. At Kellogg, as the doctor removed volumes of gravel from my underclothes, I became aware that my eye was swelling shut and requested that we pause a moment to remove my contact lenses while we could. A friend cried hysterically in the waiting room, but still a sense of quiet and calm hovered all about me.

I received a number of injuries. The top of my head felt like a water balloon. My neck and shoulders developed a lovely shade of navy blue. I must have had a swollen, fat face for a time because many days later an orderly put his head through my door with a friendly, "Well, good morning, *skinny* face!" My thighs and legs were bruised and lacerated, and several stitches were taken in my left knee. And when my back continued to go into spasms, X-rays discovered four broken transverse crosses. I slept a great deal of the time for two and a half weeks. I was aware of a constant stream of visitors—church members, fellow teachers and administrators, family, neighbors, and students all came. Their love and concern ministered deeply to me. Mail flooded in. John reported that he had received phone calls from all over the country with the message, "What's the matter up there? The Lord has been calling me to intercede for you." At home, parishioners volunteered to do baskets of ironing for me. They sent food to my family and cared for the children. The community prayed. One friend brought our youngest child, Andrea, then two, to the hospital almost every night to tuck me in. Loren, our son, came home from college to sing and play his guitar for me. I was literally inundated by love and prayer, and there was nothing I could do but lie there and learn to receive.

Even the company of heaven attended me, and I wonder now that I was not startled at the time, nor did I question what I saw. But as real as flesh-and-blood people were coming and going, there were rows of faceless figures lined up on either side of the door of my room and out into the hall. They bordered a tunnel of light that extended all the way to my bed. For a time my bed itself seemed to be covered with roses, and then the roses changed to lilies. On the wall I could see what looked like a penciled progress report— a sketch of myself looking down, looking ahead, then looking up as the days passed.

Finally there were no more mystical realities. But the embracing peace remained. I was warm inside. My emotional walls had been smashed. I *knew* the love of the Lord as healer. I was fitted with a therapeutic back brace and told I would need to wear it from six weeks to four months. I was discharged two and a half weeks after the accident, returned to school several days after that, took on an extra class, and wore the brace for only one week.

We (John writing again) share this story to follow it with others in order to show from our own lives how stubborn the heart is, how very really unconverted it is among Holy Spirit–filled, Bible-believing people, and how many ways God must move heaven and earth to reach the multifaceted diamonds of our hearts. For the first time, Paula could let people minister to her, and for the first time she could hear rebuke from me. We could have openhearted, give-and-take, real conversations. But a still unconverted level of her heart could not believe that God would be there for her. So God touched her again through the off-the-road incident as told in the previous chapter.

Paula had never known outright, purposeful sin. She had always been a "good girl." But still she remained an elder sister suffering from the elder-brother syndrome (Luke 15:11).

In the Third Baptist Church of St. Louis in which I (Paula) grew up, there was none of the judgmentalism and legalism for which some fundamentalists have come to be known. Dr. C. Oscar Johnson preached a very loving Jesus who gave Himself and died for me because He loved me. I gave myself to Him at eleven because I *knew* He loved me. I went to the altar to receive Him, solely because of love. I loved Him so much I couldn't sit through a Communion service without crying. It never dawned on me that I had never known myself as a sinner needing a Savior.

Long after Elijah House was formed and John and I were traveling all across the country to teach the love of Jesus in daily life, two Roman Catholic members of Elijah House began to confront me with a stunning, impossible word: "Paula, you don't know what it is to have a Savior."

"What do you mean, I don't know Him? I've known Him since I was eleven, and I've taught about Him for years."

"You don't know Him *as Savior*. You've never known yourself as a sinner. Only sinners can know a Savior. We feel sorry for you." (Imagine, this was coming from Catholics who were speaking to an evangelical, born-anew Baptist, no less!)

I went to John with this, and he said (doubtless with a sigh of relief), "Ask God to show you. Ask Him to reveal your flesh to you. He will." So I did.

Then one day a pastor brought a parishioner to see John, and while they were in prayer ministry, the pastor visited with me. I had difficulty believing my ears. I knew this man to be a very fine Spirit-filled pastor. Yet he was telling me in great detail about his early life as a male prostitute! I had never even heard of such a thing. But I had long practiced an unshockable manner of listening. I kept handing my reactions to the Lord silently. But I wondered why he was telling me all this. He must have repented long ago, and knew himself to be completely forgiven and made new, so why was he talking about it?

The subject changed, he left, and in the hours following I was overwhelmed with the most confusing feelings. We never locked our doors, yet I felt a compelling urge to lock all the doors and windows. I felt silly. *There's nothing threatening me*, I thought. *Why am I afraid?* Then the Holy Spirit let me know that I was trying to lock out the dawning awareness of my own *flesh*. The Lord was making me aware that the same capacity to sin is in all of us—and therefore also in me! That word registered as truth. For the first time I knew it was not because I had succeeded in being good enough that I had not fallen into gross sin—rather it was because the Lord had saved me by His grace. He had blessed me with family and upbringing and circumstances so totally unmerited that the baser part of my nature, as black as that pastor's or anyone else's, had not been so greatly tempted by opportunity to express the flesh in me. Given the same conditions, I *could* have done the same or worse as that pastor. For the first time I really saw myself as deeply sinful. It is from that base that we express sin, not as someone capable of his own righteousness who occasionally sins and so is called a *sinner*. That realization was truly humbling.

Now that I know myself as deeply sinful, I have nothing left to defend. Every once in a while, when I become too absorbed in work and not enough in devotion, my motive base subtly swings back from love to performance. God has left us a barometer. We can tell our distance from the Lord by the resurgence of striving, control, and defensiveness. Presumably He will never take performance orientation away altogether this side of heaven, and, undoubtedly, there are many more facets to the heart's diamond, still hard, rough, and unpolished.

But note the continuum: as the heart is softened, God has been able to deal with me more and more gently, from near death in a physically damaging accident, to a near accident, to words of reproof, followed by a parable in the testimony of another's life. Could that say something revealing about the change from God's ways in the Old Testament with a loving Jesus? Can it say something explanatory about our own lives? How much easier might life go if our stubborn, unbelieving hearts could hear?

That is the work of transformation and its base in evangelization, to reach anew and afresh to the countless inner unconverted areas of believers' hearts.

ACHIEVING TRANSFORMATION

How do we find the ability to transform from our performance-oriented living? It is not easy. The evil practices of the flesh are stubborn. "Therefore, since we have so great a cloud of witnesses surrounding us, let us also *lay aside every encumbrance, and the sin which so easily entangles us* [RSV says, "which *clings so closely*"], and let us run *with endurance* the race that is set before us" (Heb. 12:1, emphasis added). We are not accustomed to thinking of performance orientation, by which we strive to do so many *good* things, as sin, but it is desperately so.

First, we must make every attempt to recognize our sinful performance orientation. Allow others to speak into your life about it. Read over and over the biblical illustrations in this chapter that define it. Listen to sermon tapes that teach about it. Reread this book and others that discuss the problem.

You must come to see performance orientation not as some little series of events or as a tiny, peculiar segment of your character, but much as a metastatic cancer extending tentacles into everything you are and do. Recognize it not as some isolated little flaw, but as the very warp and woof of your entire life, and come to hate it. "Hate what is evil" (Rom. 12:9, NIV). PO is the central structure of your kingdom of self!

Repentance, metanoia in Greek, means "change, to turn around and go the other way." All such structures as performance orientation have a life of their own in us. We are created in God's image, and whatever we create within us has a life of its own and does not want to die. That evil practice within will throw smoke screens and alibis: "Oh, yeah, well, you do the same thing," or "You're not so neat yourself."

Loren used to come home feeling guilty, and knowing we had discovered some of the reasons, he would confess two or three of the maybe ten things he had done. He felt better, and so he was able to gloss over in his own conscience the other seven or eight. We thought of him as a most honest and dutifully repentant son— until we caught on. Just so, your own inner being will throw out golden apples for you to chase while the real nature of sin runs on unchecked (a parable of our inner psyche from Greek mythology).

All such structures of performance orientation carry a reward system with them. So long as we prefer the rewards, we will not change. One time I (John) kept trying and trying not to do a particular sin, praying about it over and over, only to do it again. Finally I got mad at God and cried out, "Why don't You help me with this?"

He answered quickly and succinctly, "*You aren't disgusted with it yet!*" Hate had not yet become fully ripe. God then told me, "You are still enjoying that thing."

"I do not. I hate it," I protested.

"*Son, if you hated it enough, you'd quit it. You enjoy it.*"

That led me to ask myself in what hidden ways I might in fact be enjoying sin. The Lord began to reveal mazes of subterranean lines carrying hidden delights from one pocket of pus to another. If the sin was, for example, to turn silent, cold, and inattentive around Paula, behind that single, simple happening were these roots: the delights of punishing a critical mother; feelings of power in getting another's goat; the wicked fascination of making another suffer; fantasies of being the noble martyr keeping his cool while Paula—poor thing—blows her control and becomes furious, not as able to be as "Christian and controlled" as I am; inadmissible feelings of getting even with Paula; dominance and control; male superiority—and so we could catalogue a nearly endless list of delights behind one simple sin. I am not likely to give up such rewards so long as they mean more to the hidden control centers *of my heart* than Paula or God mean to me. To come to a proper and sufficiently intense hatred of the self we have built in opposition to God is a distinct gift from the Lord. I soon discovered I couldn't hate sin enough by the power of my fleshly will to come to a true repentance. I stood helpless in corruption. "The heart is more deceitful than all else and is desperately sick; who can understand it?" (Jer. 17:9). The Latin derivative of *desperate* means "without hope," helpless.

Repentance is born of a gift of love that reaches an unrepentant, unconverted segment of our hearts. Until true love is allowed, or somehow finally touches that guarded area, we cannot change. We may set the sails of our wills determinedly again and again, but usually the first change in the winds of life finds us unable to tack— and so we *attack*. Paula and I, feeling overly responsible, have carried thousands of people in our hearts (Phil. 1:7) and worn ourselves out trying to touch that needed depth, only to discover when we let go that God could use the most unlikely circumstance (like a bike in a forty-mile-per-hour wind) or impossible person. We learned finally to believe for the other that God would touch his heart (1 Cor. 13:7, love "*believes* all things," emphasis added) and offer to be there in case the Lord wanted to touch the other through us.

If you are unable to overcome PO, you should be willing to seek the help of a Christian prayer minister or small group leader. In many cases, a prayer minister or lay leader must be willing to bear and endure (1 Cor. 13:7, love "bears all things") in patience, for the person to whom he ministers, like the drunken husband mentioned earlier, may test again and again. One lovely young lady to whom we had become father and mother in Christ wrenched our hearts again and again. One day she came to me (John) for prayer ministry and watched my face with a twinkle in her eye as this erstwhile, thoroughly moral girl told in livid detail her recent sexual experience in her first adulterous relationship. There was no way I could keep the grief out of my eyes and off my face. But I could extend forgiveness and show her that I could still love her and would still be her "father." The grief told her more than all else that I do love her.

That love and grief gave her understanding for the first time concerning how our sins grieve Jesus, and that it is not the law but our unwillingness to wound our loving Lord that keeps us from sinning. My acceptance and continued unconditional love broke through her performance orientation and told her she could rip and tear, sin and wound, and she would still be loved. The twinkle in her eye was there because she was testing me (and because of the same perverse delights I catalogued earlier when punishing Paula). Whether or not all that sin was necessary, the Lord used it to touch her heart and transform her. From that moment on she began to mature from a twenty-seven-year-old who was like an early adolescent to a lovely young woman who is today still a "daughter," but now a grown friend.

CHAPTER 4

THE BASE of LAW

The law of the LORD is perfect, restoring the soul; the testimony of the LORD is sure, making wise the simple. The precepts of the LORD are right, rejoicing the heart; the commandment of the LORD is pure, enlightening the eyes. The fear of the LORD is clean, enduring forever; the judgments of the Lord are true; they are righteous altogether. They are more desirable than gold, yes, than much fine gold; sweeter also than honey and the drippings of the honeycomb. Moreover, by them Thy servant is warned; in keeping them there is great reward.

—PSALM 19:7–11

I N AN EARLIER CHAPTER we learned that often we impute to God motives that are not His. Nowhere is that truer than in our fears relative to God and the Law. "There is no fear in love; but perfect love casts out fear, because fear involves punishment, and the one who fears is not perfected in love" (1 John 4:18). From our fear of discipline as children and our hidden resentments of authority, we may be unable to think of impersonal laws, such as the laws of sowing and reaping, discipline, and retribution, without confusing these with personal punishment or vindictiveness.

You must settle it in your heart that every law of God is the most loving gift (other than Jesus) God could give to mankind. Law describes the way love must act, or actions cease to be love. The reaping of evil seeds sown is impersonal, not personal, punishment, having nothing to do with vindictiveness or vengeance. If a man does not have a pure heart concerning childhood discipline, being unable to understand God, he cannot truly appreciate that all law is given by the Father so that man may live in blessedness.

God wants us to be happy. The "thou shalt nots" have that aim behind them, to keep us happy in a way of blessedness. It is not that God is uptight and rigid, standing in heaven with a heavy flyswatter, waiting for someone to get out of line so He can swat him to a pulp. He had to create an orderly universe for all men and nature. The universe necessarily operates on unbending principles. When we sin, we set in motion irrevocable forces. Seeing that, God "so loved the world, that He gave His only begotten Son" (John 3:16) that we might not perish.

Forgiveness does not mean that God looks the other way. It does mean that the just requirements of the Law are fulfilled in pain upon the precious body of the Lord Jesus Christ. That is how He came not to abolish the Law but to fulfill it (Matt. 5:17). He became as us in Gethsemane so that on Golgotha He could take onto Himself the full legal demands of all we set in motion (Col. 2:14). Nevertheless, the effect of that salvation often waits upon our confession, else we reap the full weight of what we have sown. It is for that precise reason that you may find yourself in need of a prayer minister or small group leader, for most often we cannot see to confess our sin without someone to help the Holy Spirit reveal it to us (James 5:13–16).

The Power for Transformation

If a small group leader knows with unwavering certainty the laws of retribution, he will know with equal certainty the power of the blood and the cross to deliver. When he assures the other of forgiveness according to the Word of God, he will not have one wisp of fear that that might not happen. He knows with absolute certainty that the blood of Jesus has in that moment washed the other clean. There is not one flicker of unrest or wondering if it will happen. It is done, finished, and unchangeable, both here and in eternity.

> My little children, I am writing these things to you that you may not sin. And if anyone sins, we have an Advocate with the Father, Jesus Christ the righteousness; and He Himself is the propitiation for our sins; and not for ours only, but also for those of the whole world.
>
> —1 John 2:1–2

> If you forgive the sins of any, their sins have been forgiven them; if you retain the sins of any, they have been retained.
>
> —John 20:23

What blessed and holy power the Lord has placed in every Christian. As a Christian, you are invested with the full power of an ambassador (2 Cor. 5:20). Heaven moves in response to the prayer of forgiveness said by the least Christian. Results are not a matter of having enough faith to make it happen. God's Word cannot lie or fail. Success is not up to the one who says the prayer. Accomplishment belongs to God, and He has declared once and for all, "It is finished" (John 19:30). It makes no difference whether you are a giant of healing or a newborn babe in Christ. God does not respect the person (Rom. 2:11), but the work and merits of His Son on the cross. Nothing in heaven or on earth could be surer than the accomplished forgiveness of God for sin upon the cross of His Son.

One of the strangest paradoxes in twenty-first-century culture is our attitude toward scientific and moral law and, therefore, our attitude toward the absoluteness of the laws foundational to Christian life and to prayer ministry. More scientists are alive today than in the sum total of all known history. Much more technology has been developed in the past few decades than was developed in several previous centuries. Knowledge has not only increased as prophesied (Dan. 12:4), but it also has rocketed far out of sight.

Whereas a man in Milton's day could lament that he had learned everything in every field available to know, now a professional man in only one limited field may find he is out of touch and that his knowledge is outdated in less than ten years, especially if he does not take constant renewal courses! Our airplanes are obsolete before they leave the drafting boards. All this has come about as mankind has gained the humility to investigate natural things and admit that some things are forever bound by natural law. "Thou hast established all the boundaries of the earth" (Ps. 74:17). All mankind, and most certainly every scientist, knows we can project rockets with precision to the boundaries of our own solar system and beyond, solely by most circumspect obedience to natural laws—with computers to help us keep on track.

If a pilot were to say, "I'm a free thinker. I think we ought to be able to land this plane upside down over there on the grass," we would not only not honor his "free thinking," but also no one would ride in anything piloted by him. Most likely if he persisted, we would send him to a mental hospital. Scientifically, freedom cannot be allowed to mean license. We rightly demand that every car be engineered and built within sound principles. The construction of every house we intend to live in must stringently obey architectural laws. It is a fair statement to assert that every technological advance we celebrate in our day owes its existence to the discovery of and obedience to precise, immutable natural laws. This most scientific of all ages is, *ipso facto,* the most law-abiding; obedience to natural law is the *sine qua non* of all science. Without obedience, nothing!

Yet the paradox is that in this most humble and obedient age relative to natural science, we have become most arrogant and deluded concerning laws that govern our hearts and spirits! We could trace historically in philosophy and semantics how such confusion has happened, but the heart's cry would be the same: "How could we ever have become so foolish!"

> For even though they knew God, they did not honor Him as God, or give thanks; but they became futile in their speculations, and their foolish heart was darkened. Professing to be wise, they became fools.
>
> —ROMANS 1:21–22

Mankind, outside the limited circles in the Church, has cast off restraint: "The kings of the earth take their stand, and the rulers take counsel against the LORD and against His Anointed: 'Let us tear their fetters apart, and cast away their cords from us!'" (Ps. 2:2–3). Many men think that all acknowledged moral laws are the fictions of men's minds, or at least only relative. Relativity, scientifically, never has meant what some have done with it in disregarding moral law. Relativity only means that each law is relative or relevant to operate within its own sphere, not that that law is not fully to be obeyed in context. The greatest scientific relativists would not dare to say that the law of gravity is not effective upon them in high places, only that it is affected by various conditions. But we in our foolishness have come to believe that "Thou shalt not commit adultery" is only relative, meaning, "not needing to be observed." When in every other sphere of natural intercourse we recognize the operation of compelling laws, how could we fail to see that, for example, in human sexual intercourse, there are laws just as immutable, just as severe, and just as irrevocable?

This is a legal universe. Every physicist knows that for every action there must be an equal and opposite reaction. Every chemist knows that every formula must balance. Even the most sexual aberrant knows life must begin with a sperm and an ovum. We see natural laws operative all about us in relation to human beings, working invincibly, unceasingly, without question. A man who does not breathe cannot live beyond physical endurance. We must eat. We must sleep. That is absolute law. Nothing changes it. We have sense enough to know that.

Nevertheless, Paula and I have ministered to many believers and even to hundreds of preachers of God's Word who think they can occasionally lie, cheat, steal, or hop in bed with anyone, and nothing will come of it! Agnes Sanford used to be fond of saying, "If you step off a cliff, you do not break the law of gravity; you illustrate it." No law of God can ever be broken! His laws work to exact retribution no matter whether we know them, mentally ignore them, choose not to observe them, feel good or bad about them, want them or hate them, believe in them and in God, or not. "Do not be deceived, God is not mocked; for whatever a man sows, this he will also reap" (Gal. 6:7). That is absolute, immutable fact.

Let men question the wisdom of our forefathers. Let men wonder whether God really said the Ten Commandments or not. Forget, if you will, the entire religious history of mankind. Discount all the Bibles, Qurans, and Rig Vedas. Does it not appall the mind that men could (apart from all these) see the controlling nature of law all around them in every sphere of human and natural existence, and not see at least by inference that the same immutability of law could pertain in spiritual and moral matters?

> For the wrath of God is revealed from heaven against all ungodliness and unrighteousness of men, who suppress the truth in unrighteousness, because that which is known about God is evident within them; for God made it evident to them. For since the creation of the world His invisible attributes,

His eternal power and divine nature, have been clearly seen, *being understood through what has been made,* so that they are without excuse.

—ROMANS 1:18–20, EMPHASIS ADDED

Incidentally, every major religion on the face of the globe contains the same basic laws we find in the Ten Commandments. God has not left Himself without witness in any age anywhere (Acts 14:17).

If rain falls down by the law of gravity, and the sun, moon, planets, and stars can swing through the universe with such precision, then is it unreasonable to assume God would take equal care to build the laws of the life of the spirit and consequent moral and ethical relationships? What a strange paradox that with firm obedience to chemical law, we fill our tanks and swallow our drugs—and think we can lie, steal, or commit adultery with impunity! It fails to make sense either scientifically or philosophically, or, forget the big words—it doesn't even make common sense the way we sometimes act!

A man with an iota of consistency to his thinking ought to be able to make a simple comparison: if a plane must fly by natural laws, so ought a marriage to "fly" solely by ethical and moral laws. Can anyone tell me how modern man can have become so paradoxical and foolish as not to know these things? The simple, horrible fact is, we have. "In whose case the god of this world has blinded the minds of the unbelieving, that they might not see the light of the gospel of the glory of Christ, who is the image of God" (2 Cor. 4:4). We are not only blinded to the Gospel, but millions also no longer can see the laws of God!

There is surely an enemy. Notwithstanding, lest we blame our foolishnesses out there somewhere, our flesh alone, without Lucifer's aid, is foolish enough. "They became futile in their speculations, and their foolish heart was darkened" (Rom. 1:21). "The mind set on the flesh is hostile toward God; for it *does not subject itself to the law of God,* for it is not even able to do so" (Rom. 8:7, emphasis added). *You see, we obey those laws of the natural order, which build our creature comforts and insure the mammon-good life, but those moral laws that haul us to account and chain our rebellious passions we want to call irrelevant, relative, man-made, or old-fashioned, anything to excuse our lusts and give them full vent!* So we reap the consequences—and wonder, in an age of knowing scientific, mechanical laws, why life doesn't go right!

GOD'S LAWS ARE FOREVER FIXED!

We must recognize this irrevocable, unbendable maxim: who would call himself a Christian must know, without a flicker of a doubt, that God's moral laws are absolutely inflexible. *Sin is sin! Law is law!* Shades of compassion and understanding relate to our comprehension of the motives for which men sin, not to the Law itself. Condemnation has no place in Christ, but that fact arrives by the mercy of the cross, never by the relaxing of any law of God.

> For truly I say to you, until heaven and earth pass away, not the smallest letter or stroke shall pass away from the Law, until all is accomplished.
>
> —MATTHEW 5:18

> Heaven and earth will pass away, but My words shall not pass away.
>
> —MATTHEW 24:35

> Whoever then annuls one of the least of these commandments, and so teaches others, shall be called least in the kingdom of heaven; but whoever keeps and teaches them, he shall be called great in the kingdom of heaven.
>
> —MATTHEW 5:19

As a small group leader or prayer minister, you do not become kind and nonjudgmental by lessening or doing away with the surety of law; you only become inept. Judgmentalism dies only as a man sees his own sin and dies in Christ to all blame, not by developing a supposed "liberal" mind.

This is an age of fleshly rationality, in which the *avant-garde* have wanted to appear magnanimous and liberal, somehow thinking man's foolish wisdom could be kinder than God's law. But "has not God made foolish the wisdom of the world?" (1 Cor. 1:20). When the light of Christ arises (Isa. 60:1–2) and the more than two thousand pigs of men's mentality have been chased into the sea, and mankind has been returned to sit fully clothed in his right mind at the feet of Jesus (Luke 8:26–39), then:

> Behold, a king shall reign in righteousness, and princes shall rule in judgment. And a man shall be as an hiding place from the wind, and a covert from the tempest; as rivers of water in a dry place, as the shadow of a great rock in a weary land. And the eyes of them that see shall not be dim, and the ears of them that hear shall hearken. The heart also of the rash shall understand knowledge, and the tongue of the stammerers shall be ready to speak plainly. The vile person shall be no more called *liberal*, nor the *churl* said to be bountiful. For the vile person will speak villany, and his heart will work iniquity, to practise hypocrisy, and to utter error against the LORD, to make empty the soul of the hungry, and he will cause the drink of the thirsty to fail. The instruments also of the *churl* are evil; he deviseth wicked devices to destroy the poor with lying words, even when the needy speaketh right. But the *liberal* deviseth liberal things; and by *liberal* things shall he stand.
>
> —ISAIAH 32:1–8, KJV, EMPHASIS ADDED

The laws of God are forever fixed, no matter what our puny minds may be tempted to think or whatever sins are paraded by the silly speculations of this deluded world. God calls all men to awaken to the truth of God's shining principles ribbing all of life with sure pillars to live by. Psalm 119 should be the believer's constant song of covenant. We must be passionately in love with the law of God, meditating on it day and night (Ps. 1:2).

The Life of the Lay Leader

As for the prayer minister or lay leader—if you are not dead sure that God's Word is absolute, His laws given by revelation, and that He meant what He said, get out of ministry before you do more harm! I mean that with every fiber of my being! Countless times Paula and I have listened with great grief to troubled souls whose lives were even more wrecked by foolish advice: "Have an affair." Or, "Don't feel so guilty." Or, "That's just old-fashioned nonsense." Or, "Surely you don't believe that stuff anymore, do you?" What judgment such lay leaders are heaping up for the day of reckoning: "Let not many of you become teachers, my brethren, knowing that as such we shall incur a stricter judgment" (James 3:1). "But whoever causes one of these little ones who believe in Me to stumble, it is better for him that a heavy millstone be hung around his neck, and that he be drowned in the depth of the sea. Woe to the world because of its stumbling blocks! For it is inevitable that stumbling blocks come; but woe to that man through whom the stumbling block comes!" (Matt. 18:6–7).

The personal life of a prayer minister or lay leader must be impeccable. Perhaps no other office in the church is more subject to temptation. Those who enter the inner chambers of people's secret hearts, to yearn and wrestle for them, cannot help becoming contaminated by the person's emotions and sometimes somewhat overburdened with their cares and sorrows. A lay leader must know by the Word of God how to detach himself and cut himself free from burdens: "For wisdom is protection just as money is protection. But the advantage of knowledge is that wisdom preserves the lives of its possessors" (Eccles. 7:12). Whoever does not cherish and wed himself eternally to God's law in Christ is described by Proverbs 25:28 (KJV): "He that hath no rule over his own spirit is like a city that is broken down, and without walls."

A lay leader's personal devotional life is his salvation. Only the Lord can cleanse the gunk and lift the load of people out of his heart and spirit. Only love, often renewed at the fountain of life (Ps. 36:9), can cause his love for obedience to the Law to be born continually from the love of Jesus flowing through him to others. The love that flows from the throne of God is like a river (Rev. 22:1; Ps. 46:4). A leader loves the Law because it provides sure banks for the river of that love to flow in its own channel. If a leader does not keep up his own devotional life, the river will run dry, his heart will become barren and brittle, and the Law will become a whip to scourge others rather than banks for the river of God's love.

A lay leader's personal moral life must be above reproach, not only for his own sake but also for the security of those to whom he ministers. If we do not grasp the eternal reality of the Law and the grievous price Jesus paid for us on the cross, Satan can use the melee of the battle to put blinders on our eyes until we no longer see the consequences of what we do, nor will we have a conscience that works as it should. Then, though we began well, we will become lost from the Lord in the midst of the battle—and become blinded.

But I am not speaking just to those who minister, for the thesis of this book is that the entire body of Christ is called to minister. But let me distinguish carefully, for I am not calling any Christian to be a psychologist. Any of us may use psychological insights and be grateful for them. But our base is not the same.

PSYCHOLOGY VS. FAITH

Psychology takes its origin from Descartes, a French philosopher (1596–1650) who said, "*Cognito, ergo sum,*" or "I think, therefore I am." That makes our life dependent on what we have been trained to think rather than on the fact that we have an immortal spirit and soul. Faith maintains that we have a spirit, which by personal choices forms a soul in which are character and personality. Christian faith says, "God speaks, and we hear." And it adds that our spirits can intuitively grasp knowledge far beyond the mind, even without God's help.

Parapsychology regards extrasensory perception, kinesis, clairaudience, clairvoyance, psychometry, and other related phenomena as functions of the psyche. Thus psychology examines only two levels of human existence. Faith embraces a trichotomy of mind, heart, and spirit. Faith says that the conscious mind and heart are informed, guided, sometimes controlled, and surely greatly influenced by the deep mind and heart of our spirit.

Psychologists who are Skinnerian behaviorists (based on determinism) attempt to change people by giving them "modes" or ways of changing the way they behave. Social actionists think that if they can lobby to change laws to improve society and thus spread a good environment to every person, they will have effected change to bring about the brotherhood of mankind. Christians may lend support to some social actions, and prayer ministers may employ some Skinnerian modes for self-discipline, but Christians see no lasting change by any other means than changing the *inner* heart by reaching the spirit with conviction of guilt, confession, and forgiveness. We are not changed from outside in but from the inside out.

Psychological method is enlightenment, to know one's *self*. Christian method is enlightenment, to know one's self as *sinful*. Psychologists attempt to encourage change by intention or willpower to make a better person. Christian power is first the Holy Spirit, secondly prayer, to make a *converted* person. Psychologists try to change the environment, the way the family behaves, or the circumstances (like the way the house is kept or job stresses or the companions around us). A prayer minister or lay leader, seeing such actions as somewhat helpful, seeks first to change inner attitudes and motives toward persons and circumstances by forgiveness and the indwelling, loving nature of Jesus. A prayer minister or lay leader may not attempt to change the circumstances at all, seeing those as the milieu in which the Lord intends to write on the person's heart whatever lessons God knows he needs to learn.

A psychologist has his eyes on function, attempting to restore the counselee to capacity to act. Prayer ministry, though eventually wanting the individual to be able to function, seeks first to enable the person to be convicted in his heart.

Thus in ministry we work to establish guilt. We are not afraid of it, and unless we perceive false guilt, we would never suggest, "Don't feel guilty." Unless a person recognizes guilt, that person's sin cannot find its way to the cross, and freedom cannot happen.

Some psychologists, relying too much on the deterministic approach, too often look upon persons as victims rather than perpetrators. Life has happened to them. Cultural determinism means that life has done to us what we are. Thus criminals are "not responsible." We (society) have created them. Consequently, some psychologists have produced self-pitying persons who are sure that life has done upon them all their troubles. Karl Menninger, a great contemporary psychiatrist, has hauled secular psychology to account for its failure in this area in his book *Whatever Became of Sin?* from which we quote: "The message is simple. It is that concern is the touchstone. Caring. Relinquishing the sin of indifference. This recognizes acedia as the Great Sin; the heart of all sin. Some call it selfishness. Some call it alienation. Some call it schizophrenia. Some call it egocentricity. Some call it separation."[1]

Power for change for psychologists is found in natural desire and human willpower, plus counsel and the support of friends and relatives. Power for change for Christians is first faith in the power and intentions of God as expressed through His Son, our Lord Jesus Christ upon the cross, through His blood and resurrection life, followed by other helps the Holy Spirit inspires.

Thus we are not calling members of the body of Christ to be psychologists, but rather to be confessors, midwives, and fathers and mothers in Christ to one another in the body of Christ. We are calling the body to deal with the common daily problems of life in a biblical, concrete manner of ministry and prayer.

If one truly grasps the few simple laws on which God has constructed the operation of human nature, that single key is enough to begin to unlock the myriad mysteries of the human heart! Human nature, like car engines, operates on absolute mechanical principles. Once one understands the base of law behind all human relationships, he has the foundation on which to build and plumb perceptions into every problem. The genius of Einstein was to discover the simplicity of law behind the seemingly complex construction of nature. The genius of the Word of God is to lay bare the simplicity of life. It is as though all life, like fractions, is built on simple common denominators upon which operate multivarious numerators. If a Christian is sufficiently gripped by the simple statutes of God, his eyes will never be blinded by the kaleidoscopic variations of human complexities. Beneath all he will see and return to the simple keys. The numerators (how we see and act) vary as often as there are individuals who mess up. The denominators (the laws of God) are few, basic, universal, and simple.

God gives us the single basic key to life in the Ten Commandments and the Sermon on the Mount. Those moral laws are not somebody's guess as to how life ought to run. They are not mankind's invention. We did not learn them by trial and error. They are not merely a bunch of rules that if only everybody would obey, this would be a better world. They are *God's description of the way reality works.* The Ten Commandments and the Sermon on the Mount are the architect's blueprint for building the house of family life. They are the chemist's formula for brewing safe mixtures of men and women. They are the engineer's principles for construction and operation of all relationships. They are the cook's recipe for nurture, not poison.

They are not inert, negligible things. If a man leaves his car in the garage, the only harm is that he hitches rides or walks and pays his car bills for nothing. But if a man parks the Ten Commandments in the garage of forgetfulness, he will sooner or later reap a whirlwind of destruction.

Many people think that the Ten Commandments and the Sermon on the Mount are some nice idealist's list of *shoulds*, but that, of course, the practically minded macho man knows better. Many think that not to know a commandment or to neglect or disregard one is of no more consequence than a liberating philosophical exercise, affecting nothing other than an overactive conscience. A strange fact is that not one of these same "practically minded" people would ever think he could walk into a room full of tear gas and expect that his ignorance of it or neglect to wear a mask could have no effect! God's laws are like a thousand-mile-an-hour gale; given time they will sweep everything before them, even as a thousand-mile-an-hour wind will eventually wear down a mountain. Anyone who has watched a mighty flood uproot a tree or hurl a house like a toothpick has a tiny approximation of the power of God's laws. A wind will stop and a flood will cease, but God's laws will continue to operate beyond the pale of death throughout eternity.

The truth is that the "practically minded" man is blinded and deluded.

> Because the sentence against an evil deed is not executed quickly, therefore the hearts of the sons of men among them are given fully to do evil.
> —ECCLESIASTES 8:11

The mills of God's justice grind slowly, but they grind exceedingly fine. Because the "practical man" does not see immediate retribution, he fails to believe. That unbelief has no effect whatsoever upon the operation of God's law; he and his descendants will reap without fail no matter what he thinks or disbelieves, is aware of or rejects. Note again, even in Christians of long standing, we are dealing with unbelief in the heart. Millions upon millions of Christians have never yet become so grounded in God's Word that His law is written indelibly into their hearts (Jer. 31:33). In the heart they still believe they can do whatever they want with no effect. It is as though the strands of consistency are all snapped, swaying in the scattering winds of fleshly lusts and desires. They do not and cannot effectively connect cause and effect, sowing and reaping, sin and result, or good deed and blessing.

Every Christian who ministers to another must consequently never let himself assume that the other person effectively holds to the laws of God or to right and wrong. The mind of the person being guided may give lip service, but "this people honors Me with their lips, but their heart is far away from Me" (Matt. 15:8). Every Christian is therefore constantly an evangelist and teacher *to the heart*. Men simply do not connect sin and retribution *in the heart and life* in real and practical terms.

> And when He approached, He saw the city and wept over it, saying, "If you had known in this day, even you, the things which make for peace! But now they have been hidden from your eyes."
>
> —Luke 19:41–42

"Honor Your Father and Your Mother"

The fundamental, simple, and single key to prayer ministry or small group ministry is found in the fifth commandment: "Honor your father and your mother, as the Lord your God has commanded you, that your days may be prolonged, and that it may go well with you on the land which the Lord your God gives you" (Deut. 5:16). That single principle, that life will go well with those who honor their parents and that life will not go well with those who do not, goes far to explain *the cause* of most marital problems, child-rearing dilemmas, and moral and immoral inclinations. That single fifth commandment is a description in all human life of the way reality works. In every area consciously or unconsciously that we judged or dishonored our parents, in that very area life will not go well with us!

Life is that fundamentally simple.

> Even so, every good tree bears good fruit; but the bad tree bears bad fruit. A good tree cannot produce bad fruit, nor can a bad tree produce good fruit. Every tree that does not bear good fruit is cut down and thrown into the fire. So then, you will know them by their fruits.
>
> —MATTHEW 7:17–20

> Do not judge lest you be judged. For in the way you judge, you will be judged; and by your standard of measure, it shall be measured to you.
>
> —MATTHEW 7:1–2

> Do not be deceived, God is not mocked; for whatever a man sows, this he will also reap.
>
> —GALATIANS 6:7

Those few simple laws encompass every human relationship. There is no escape. There are no exceptions. Life will without fail go the way of not only our good deeds, but also our sins, judgments, and sowings, unless the grace of Christ intervenes.

When we are ministering to another, once we settle in our minds that we are not dealing with fantasy or myth but with eternal, unchangeable reality that will outlast all the universe, we cannot be carried away into suppositions and fallacies (Ps. 119:89). We have the unfailing key to truth. For example, an individual may say, "Oh, I couldn't help doing this or that wrong thing to my mate." When overcorrecting, scolding, and criticizing, he may rationalize it by saying, "I just learned from my parents that there is a right way to do things, and if a thing is worth doing, it's worth doing right. And

I love my husband (wife) so, I just want him (her) to do the best he (she) can, so everything will go right for us."

A good tree cannot produce bad fruit. To demand and control is bad fruit; it is impossible for that to arise from love. Love is good. Control is bad. That bad fruit had to have come from some bad root in the person's life. Perhaps the father or mother criticized, nagged, and controlled. The child hated it but thought it was not acceptable to feel angry with parents. Not understanding the phrase "be angry, and…do not sin" (Eph. 4:26), the child repressed such feelings. Now the law (Rom. 2:1) compels the adult to nag and criticize in the same manner as it was done to him (her).

So often we want to ascribe our rotten behavior to good things in us. Understanding of the pristine clarity of God's laws reveals man's lies to himself. The purity of law threads the eye of every needle and unties the Gordian knots of human character. The law of God pierces webs of deception. "The commandment of the LORD is pure, enlightening the eyes" (Ps. 19:8). "The unfolding of Thy words gives light; it gives understanding to the simple" (Ps. 119:130).

There are plenty of maybes in our understanding of problems, and every lay minister ought to be clothed with humility and willingness to admit error. "The first to plead his case seems just, until another comes and examines him" (Prov. 18:17). But there are no maybes in the operation of law. Our understandings are faulty, but the swing of retribution in the realities we examine is without elasticity or change. Only the grace of Christ on the cross stops the swing of inevitable retribution.

Therefore when God reveals, we need to believe and act with prayer to deliver. We cannot do that if we are "tossed here and there by waves, and carried about by every wind of doctrine, by the trickery of men, by craftiness in deceitful scheming" (Eph. 4:14). It is firm belief in the law of God that pinions our mind to the secure foundations of life.

To those not so firmly secured, we should say, "No, if you can't release your child to go to college, it is not because you 'love him too much.' Possession is bad fruit. Love is good. Good trees can't produce bad fruit. Now let's find out the real reason why you can't let him go."

To the man experiencing marital problems: "You love your wife too much; therefore, you say you couldn't help beating up on that guy who looked at her at the party? No, my friend. Love, being good, produces no bad fruit. Bad fruit has to come from bad roots in a bad tree. Now who left whom in your childhood, or who kept taking something away that was yours? What happened between your father and mother, or with your brothers and sisters? Somewhere there was a bad experience. Let's find it."

A person cannot say, "He would have left me. I had to go to bed with him. I love him too much, I guess." Never allow a noble reason behind an ignoble thing. That is impossible. Good trees don't produce bad fruit.

As a minister, you might say, "Not so, honey. Love, being good, doesn't produce sin. We try to use love to cloak sin, but something else produced it. What were you afraid of? Let's look at your relationship to your father. What kind of job did he have? Was he home at night? Was he 'home' when he was home? Did he stay with your mother? How did they get along? Most importantly, how might you have judged them?"

Have you begun to see how the Word of God is a protection to the mind of a minister—or anyone else? "How can a young man keep his way pure? By keeping it according to Thy word" (Ps. 119:9). "Thy Word I have *treasured in my heart,* that I may not sin against Thee" (v. 11, emphasis added). "Every word of God is tested; He is a shield to those who take refuge in Him" (Prov. 30:5).

To the person who ministers to another, the Word of God is a sure sword of analysis, not psychological tests or gimmicks. That is what the Holy Spirit Himself says it is:

For the word of God is living and active and sharper than any two-edged sword, and piercing as far as the division of soul and spirit, of both joints and marrow, and *able to judge the thoughts and intentions of the heart.*

—HEBREWS 4:12, EMPHASIS ADDED

Then you will discern righteousness and justice and equity and every good course. For wisdom will enter your heart, and knowledge will be pleasant to your soul; discretion will guard you, understanding will watch over you, to deliver you from the way of evil, from the man who speaks perverse things; from those who leave the path of uprightness, to walk in the ways of darkness; who delight in doing evil, and rejoice in the perversity of evil; whose paths are crooked, and who are devious in their ways.

—PROVERBS 2:9–15

Whether we are allowing God to deal with the hidden roots of sin in our own hearts or ministering to another believer with the expectation of transformation, we must be like detectives, seeking for the real "who-done-its" in each hidden corner. The Word of God is a sure magnifying glass, and just as every fingerprint uniquely nails the culprit, so the Law reveals precisely the stamp of each man's nature. Be sure that your heart and mind are rooted in the singleness of God's Word. "The lamp of the body is the eye; if therefore your eye is clear, your whole body will be full of light" (Matt. 6:22). The "eye" is the way we interpret life—it must be single, captive to the Word of God (2 Cor. 10:5).

Therefore, since we have this ministry, as we received mercy, we do not lose heart, but we have renounced the things hidden because of shame, not walking in craftiness or adulterating the word of God, but by the manifestation of truth commending ourselves to every man's conscience in the sight of God.

—2 CORINTHIANS 4:1–2

Our life with our parents, or whoever raised us, is the root and trunk of our life. Whatever manifests in the present derives from those roots. After forty years of doing prayer ministry for as many as twelve hundred hours in each year, Paula and I can confidently and restfully say that ministry is at root that simple, and the Law of God is that basic.

It is not that parents are to blame. Whatever parents were, saints or hellions, normal people or psychos, what is important is the child's reactions. We have seen cases of children who were hellishly abused yet nevertheless became loving and gentle adults. We are not dealing with cultural determinism, or behaviorism, which puts forth that man is formed by his circumstances, by environment, and by people. We are comprehending by the Word of God, which proclaims that by our spirit we have chosen how we will react. In every way we have reacted sinfully, we have set in motion forces that must be reaped, unless mercy prevails. We do not blame parents by seeing that the root and trunk of all life is formed with them. We must always bear our own load of guilt (Gal. 6:5).

Placing guilt on a two-year-old does not place blame or condemnation. In Christ that is ruled out (Rom. 8:1). We see the facts of the operation of law in order to deliver by the cross. We are not interested in finding out whose fault (whose blame) anything is. We *are* interested in seeing what events and what reactions happened, and what resultant character structures were built, so that we can take the result of sin to the cross. Once we see that every human being is sinful by inheritance, blame dies. We might justly attach blame to someone who, as Paul says, has already been cleansed and filled by the Holy Spirit and who then purposely chooses evil, and thus chooses to crucify Jesus anew (Heb. 6:6). But in dealing with the normal sinfulness of us all, blame is not a part of the game. It is totally irrelevant, like a player who never got into the ballpark, much less up to bat. All of us have been born with sinful hearts into a sinful world.

> He has not dealt with us according to our sins, nor rewarded us according to our iniquities.... Just as a father has compassion on his children, so the LORD has compassion on those who fear Him. For He Himself knows our frame; He is mindful that we are but dust.
>
> —Psalm 103:10, 13–14

It might seem that we have said on the one hand that every man is responsible for choosing wrongly, and that now we say that every man is born sinful, thus inferring he had no chance. Not so; every man is indeed responsible for his choices. We are guilty. But our diminished state is so deep and pervasive that we are capable of developing sin structures of which we are unaware. Jesus said, "Father, forgive them; for they do not know what they are doing" (Luke 23:34). But compassion says that although every man is held accountable, the compassion of the Lord does not blame and condemn him. For those who are made aware of a root of bitterness and choose to repent, it only loves and delivers.

The absoluteness of the law of God also becomes the surety of healing:

> For when God made the promise to Abraham, since He could swear by no one greater, He swore by Himself, saying, "I will surely bless you, and I will surely multiply you." And thus, having patiently waited, he obtained the promise. For men swear by one greater than themselves, and with them an oath given as confirmation is an end of every dispute. In the same way God, desiring even more to *show to the heirs of the promise the unchangeableness of His purpose,* interposed with an oath, in order that *by two unchangeable things, in which it is impossible for God to lie, we may have strong encouragement,* we who have fled for refuge in *laying hold of the hope* set before us. This hope we have *as an anchor* of the soul, a hope both sure and *steadfast* and one which enters within the veil, where Jesus

has entered as a forerunner for us, having become a high priest forever according to the order of Melchizedek.

—HEBREWS 6:13–20, EMPHASIS ADDED

ARROGANCE OR HUMILITY?

Here is one final word of clarification and comfort for you, whether or not you have yet recognized God's calling to you to be a prayer minister or lay leader. You desire to stand upon the absoluteness of God's Word yet fear the threat of being called *narrow, bigoted, arrogant, opinionated,* or *foolish.* Satan and our confused modern mentality have completely turned things backward, making crooked the straight paths of God (Acts 13:10). Men in the world call arrogant that which is humility, and vice versa. For example, in the face of all the amassed evidence of scientific endeavor, if a man were to stubbornly insist that the world is flat, we would not call that man anything but arrogant and foolish, would we? Considering the evidence, to admit that the earth is round is humility. To believe that fact unreservedly is not arrogance or narrowness; it is to have a sound mind (2 Tim. 1:7, KJV). To settle the roundness of the earth as something proven beyond doubt is to possess the flexibility to change any erstwhile contrary opinions, and the sense to lock the mind firmly onto reality. It is the same concerning the absoluteness of God's Word.

In the beginning, to accept the finality of God's Word may have to be taken as one would a scientific hypothesis. One tests it and wonders if he has taken leave of his senses. Whoever so puts God to the test (Mal. 3:10) and obeys His statutes will soon discover that God confirms by signs and wonders (Mark 16:17) and that "in the mouth of two or three witnesses shall every word be established" (2 Cor. 13:1, KJV). The confirmation of God will soon become such a mountain of evidence that not to believe and settle it once and for all would be the height of mental arrogance, narrowness, and foolishness.

Once it is seen that in His revealed and written Word God has indeed spoken once and for all, that sight so overturns the world's way of thinking that it becomes humility to admit His absolutes to the core of all our thinking and arrogance to continue to parade upon the ground of man's fleshly speculations. Christians who *know* the absolutes of God's laws need not fear; it takes a humble mind to be settled honestly upon the truth of God's Word and an arrogant mind not to be so settled.

CHAPTER 5

THE CENTRAL POWER
AND NECESSITY
OF FORGIVENESS

And whenever you stand praying, forgive, if you have anything against anyone; so that your Father also who is in heaven may forgive you your transgressions. But if you do not forgive, neither will your Father who is in heaven forgive your transgressions.

—MARK 11:25–26

THE FIRST NECESSITY OF forgiveness derives from the Law. Until forgiveness is effected in the heart, the law of retribution swings to its inevitable conclusion: "When lust is conceived, it gives birth to sin; and when sin is accomplished, it brings forth death" (James 1:15). The legality of the universe demands resolution.

The Cause and Effect of Emotional Stimuli

Every anger in a family is a stimulus. Every stimulus engenders response, whether we acknowledge it consciously or repress it. Each response becomes stimulus to the other, in turn demanding response, which becomes stimulus, demanding further response, and so arguments incite to fights, group hassles to riots, and national tensions to wars. "What is the source of quarrels and conflicts among you? Is not the source your pleasures that wage war in your members? You lust and do not have; so you commit murder. And you are envious and cannot obtain; so you fight and quarrel" (James 4:1–2).

As long as we remain unrepentant of a bitter root, our response to an emotional stimulus will illustrate the law of sowing and reaping. This law will operate as legally as the laws of electricity. We may try to control our passions, break the stimulus-response arc by willpower or kindly character, or withhold further stimuli by suppressing our own responses, but we only delay, for there are lawful impetuses that cannot be denied. We *will* reap what is sown (Gal. 6:7). God's laws (His Word) cannot be broken (John 10:35).

That fact of the immutability of law is the truth of what the Holy Spirit said in Malachi 3:6: "For I, the Lord, do not change; therefore you, O sons of Jacob, are *not consumed*" (emphasis added). If God changed, we *would* be consumed. If He changed what? "Hence, also, He is able to save forever those who draw near to God through Him, since He *always lives to make intercession for them*" (Heb. 7:25, emphasis added). The logic is inescapable—if Jesus changed and thus stopped interceding before the Father, the result would be, "This tape will self-destruct in five seconds!"

The laws of sowing and reaping and of increase ensure that all our human relationships, indeed all of human life, because of our continually sinning flesh, must be ever accelerating to war and destruction! Nothing can stop that swing, save the cross of Christ. That is the centrality of forgiveness: "And according to the Law, one may almost say, all things are cleansed with blood, and without shedding of blood there is no forgiveness" (Heb. 9:22). Hate murders: "Everyone who hates his brother is a murderer; and you know that no murderer has eternal life abiding in him" (1 John 3:15). All resentments and bitternesses are born of hate; no matter how we may want to euphemize and claim we don't hate, we do. Our emotions murder (or bless) the other. Murder destroys life. Life is in the blood (Gen. 9:4). Unless sinful propensities born of bitter roots are repented of, stimulus demands response, and seed sown requires reaping; therefore, every hatred requires blood. Only the blood of Jesus can enable us to die to self, and stop the increasing cycle of human hate. The blood of forgiveness is thus central even to the possibility of continuance of human life.

When Mary Jones feels slighted by her husband, Sam, her unresolved bitterness toward others who have slighted her in the past demands a response. If she vents it, he might respond out of his own bitterness. Anger increases, and battle ensues. If he suppresses, that stimulus does not die. It ferments in his heart. Somewhere, somehow, it *will* express, even if only by silent rejection, while subliminally, Sam's bitterness is unknowingly murdering his wife. Sam may, by fleshly determination, or even by the power of the Holy Spirit, give back a loving answer, and that may evoke a loving response, and so the evening may spiral to joy. Nevertheless, that original hurt cannot be denied. If it is not properly expressed and dealt with, it lives, repressed and forgotten. But the universe is legal, and that hurt must yet find a response.

If we multiply that event by the thousands that normally occur in any relationship, we see that if Jesus failed to intercede continually, death of happiness, or even physical destruction, is unavoidable for all of us. Today, as the world has turned more and more from God, His mercy is prevented. We hear news reports so much more often of people shooting and killing one another. The cycle of hate swings to death unhindered by grace. Law is law, and reaping is inevitable when grace is prevented.

"But if we walk in the light as He Himself is in the light, we have fellowship with one another, and the blood of Jesus His Son cleanses us from all sin" (1 John 1:7). Sam's choice to love was an invitation, by choosing to walk in light, to allow the blood of Jesus to cleanse the heart.

On the other hand, no one can know how many billions of instances flow to wholeness every day in human relationships by His blood, all unseen and unknown. How overwhelmingly gracious our Lord's mercy is, no one can ever know! Nor can anyone know why so many billions of incidents can wash unknown in the blood, though on the other hand, sometimes conscious recognition and confession are required, else we suffer the full consequences. Surely God, in His wisdom, knows. Most sins apparently are cleansed without our ever knowing. Suffice it to say that the command, "Do this in remembrance of me" (Luke 22:19), is probably based on Jesus' knowledge of our continuous need of washing. How often does God forgive and cleanse us as we worship and we are not aware of it? Choices to walk in love cleanse, but the most effective choices are worship and prayer. We need to pray for one another regularly, as did St. Paul, "May the God of peace Himself *sanctify* you entirely; and may your spirit and soul and body be *preserved* complete, *without blame* at the coming of our Lord Jesus Christ" (1 Thess. 5:23, emphasis added). What a prayer!

THE IMPORTANCE OF COMMUNION AND WORSHIP

Having been privileged as perhaps few others to see daily into the inner workings of the human heart, Paula and I both rejoice and grieve over the scriptures:

> Let us hold fast the confession of our hope without wavering,
> for He who promised is faithful; and let us consider how to

stimulate one another to love and good deeds, *not forsaking our own assembling together,* as is the habit of some, but encouraging one another; and all the more, as you see the day drawing near. For if we go on sinning willfully after receiving the knowledge of the truth, there *no longer remains a sacrifice for sins,* but a certain terrifying expectation of judgment, and the fury of a fire *which will consume* the adversaries.

—HEBREWS 10:23–27, EMPHASIS ADDED

We rejoice because we know that those who do attend worship, whether Communion is served or not, will be cleansed by walking in the light, and their marriages and families will be blessed whether or not they know it. Families may battle upon exit from the church doors, but much of that prior week's accumulation of seeds sown to hate has been reaped by our Lord. People may remember angers and call them into new battles, but the necessary legal retribution of the past was effectually ended at the cross in worship.

We weep as we see the grayness of death come over the faces of those who never darken His door; we know what horrendous accumulations of evil rebound to resolution in reaping because they have failed that opportunity to choose life in Him, and thus gave Him little opportunity to cleanse.

The power of forgiveness is the blood of Jesus. And the blood of Jesus is sufficient (Heb. 10:19–29). We doubt that the Church could get "bloody" enough. Simon Menno (1496–1561), from whom the Mennonites were spawned, was noted both for his piety and for his emphasis upon the blood of Jesus—an emphasis that was inherited by his followers. While on board a ship bound for America in 1735, John Wesley was so influenced by the gracious piety of a party of Moravians, who sang of the blood of Jesus, that from that beginning many believe came his impetus into revival, and from that experience early Methodism was filled with piety and songs of celebration of the blood of Jesus.

A cursory check through American church history reveals that wherever piety and celebration of the blood of Jesus have *preceded,* so also have *proceeded* revival and true loving life in our Lord Jesus Christ. It is the blood of Jesus that sprinkles the heart, the arena of inner space we need to conquer: "And since we have a great priest over the house of God, let us draw near with a sincere heart in full assurance of faith, having our *hearts sprinkled clean from an evil conscience* and our bodies washed with pure water" (Heb. 10:21– 22, emphasis added). How often have we sung, "Draw me nearer, nearer, nearer, blessed Lord, to Thy precious bleeding side," and did not know the power of what we sang?[1]

May every Christian never forget the greatest tool of power God has placed in his hands—the blood of Jesus. The Word of God is given for a mighty tool, for it is "the power of God for salvation" (Rom. 1:16). But the blood of Jesus is the foremost power for the cleansing of the heart: "And to Jesus, the mediator of a new covenant, and to the sprinkled blood, which speaks better than the blood of Abel [which cried to the Father from the ground]" (Heb. 12:24).

> Therefore even the first covenant was not inaugurated without blood. For when every commandment had been spoken by Moses to all the people according to the Law, he took the blood of the calves and the goats, with water and scarlet wool and hyssop, and sprinkled both the book itself and all the people, saying, *"This is the blood of the covenant which God commanded you."* And in the same way he sprinkled both the tabernacle and all the vessels of the ministry with the blood. And according to the Law, one may almost say, all things are cleansed with blood, and without shedding of blood there is no forgiveness. Therefore, it was necessary for the copies of the things in the heavens to be cleansed with these, but the heavenly things themselves with better sacrifices than these. For Christ did not enter a holy place made with hands, a mere copy of the true one, but into heaven itself, now to appear in

the presence of God for us; nor was it that He should offer Himself often, as the high priest enters the holy place year by year with blood not his own. Otherwise, He would have needed to suffer often since the foundation of the world; but now once at the consummation He has been manifested to put away sin by the sacrifice of Himself. And inasmuch as it is appointed for men to die once, and after this comes judgment; so Christ also, having been offered once to bear the sins of many, shall appear a second time for salvation without reference to sin, to those who eagerly await Him.

—HEBREWS 9:18–28, EMPHASIS ADDED

The blood of Jesus is central to the healing of the human heart. The Word corrects *the mind* and *pierces to the heart* (Heb. 4:12), but it is the blood that heals the heart. The paradox is that though that blood once offered need never be offered again, its application is daily required, or the heart sickens and sours anew. We cannot by logic or willpower change the heart. No matter how clearly we see what lodges there, there it remains. Here is where the secular psychologist stands bankrupt, for he cannot cleanse what he sees. But the Christian can. Where the secular leaves off, the Christian has only begun. We have but to call for the blood of the Lamb: "Behold, the Lamb of God [our perfect blood sacrifice] who *takes away the sin of the world!*" (John 1:29, emphasis added).

The prayer takes no measure of faith, only enough to voice the asking. The least Christian wields the fullness of power. How indescribably great that though sins multiply as darkness increases, we can never exhaust the blood of Jesus! His faithfulness guarantees that it is always there, at the nearest asking, to cleanse the heart thoroughly and completely.

Learn to "Fly Blind"

The greatest difficulty concerning forgiveness is that most often we do not know we still cherish resentment or that we have lied to ourselves and forgotten. You must not base conviction of sin or lack of it on feeling like you have forgiven. Feelings about such issues are inveterate liars at best. Thoughts and memories are glossed over with euphemisms and lies such as: "I was never angry." "It didn't hurt." The key was given in the last chapter: if a bad fruit exists, a hidden unforgiveness must lie at the root. It is the clean logic of the Word of God that brings to light the hidden sins of your heart, not your own confused notions and feelings about yourself.

Pilots must go through intensive training to retrain the mind not to adhere to their own senses of up and down, light and dark, but to believe the instruments and lock coordination into flying "blind." "Who is blind but My servant, or so deaf as My messenger whom I send? Who is so blind as he that is at peace with Me, or so blind as the servant of the Lord?" (Isa. 42:19). "And He will *not judge by what His eyes see, nor make a decision by what His ears hear*" (Isa. 11:3, emphasis added).

Prayer ministers and lay leaders must learn to fly blind, trusting only the instrument of God's Word, not men's senses or feelings. "The law of the Lord is perfect, *restoring the soul;* the testimony of the Lord is sure, *making wise the simple*" (Ps. 19:7, emphasis added). Though we laid down these understandings as basic in the last chapter, let us now see that nowhere are they more true and incisive in application than in the matter of forgiveness. People almost invariably think they have forgiven when they haven't. And how shall we know? By simple, pure logic according to God's Word. If the problem is still there, forgiveness is incomplete.

That's why it is often necessary to be ministered to or to minister to another who is seeking transformation from hidden sins. It is one thing for a person who is ministering to another to see the problem;

it is another thing altogether for the one receiving ministry to allow his heart, as well as his mind, to do so.

Remember that although the Law is absolute, there are no certainties in comprehension. Never say to the person to whom you are ministering, "Aha, you have this or that problem." Rather, invite the other—by question, parables, stories, and so forth—to recognize what has been hidden in his heart. Search out the whole history of the person, and don't leap to premature conclusions. Invite that person to search to see and connect things within himself.

HOW DO WE DEAL WITH THE PAST?

Many people confusedly think that they have to go back and find whoever the person or event was that precipitated the root of sin and talk it out. This is not even possible if that person has died. It may not only be unnecessary to talk to the person in question, but also hurtful. Whoever hurt us may be unaware, or if aware thought it long ago forgiven and done with. Forgiveness can be accomplished purely within the hidden heart of the believer. It may be that the Holy Spirit will later prompt you to take part in a present-day talk and reconciliation, but this should only be done with wisdom and with tact. It is not always necessary.

When parents were normal and good, it is strangely more difficult to get at roots than when parents were recognizably evil. Resentments in the latter case are easily seen and admitted consciously. But loyalty masks the other, both in childhood and as a grown believer desiring transformation. Here again, the straight, clean logic of the Word enables us to act on faith, disregarding feelings, as Paula and I have testified earlier.

Frequently, resentments lie totally beneath both the heart and mind, having originated so early that we sometimes cannot remember, or from reactions to things left undone by those who ought to have done them for us. Sometimes parents have almost never done anything demonstrably evil, and yet have almost failed as parents. One instance occurs in homes in which parents were God-fearing, moral, upstanding, dutiful people, but they never touched the children with affection. The children's minds and hearts could not know what was lacking and remembered only the good things the parents did. But their spirits ached for touch and resented its lack. Now the adult cannot give love, and the family is starving. Perhaps the mate is unfaithful. Bad fruit evidences the bitter root. Prayer for forgiveness delivers where no resentment has ever been consciously felt.

Another example is most tragic. We have often ministered to people whose parents not only did almost everything correctly, but they also gave copious affection; yet they failed miserably as parents. Why? Because they did not know how to give the child space to be his own person. They so overdid things that they snuffed out the budding life of the child. Such children as adults may have extreme difficulty seeing resentment as a base in their hearts in their present difficulties. Again the present fruit of a fearful, squashed life reveals the presence of a bad root of resentment in the spirit of the child. Repentance, confession, and absolution must be solely by faith according to the Word of God.

Events are not what we are primarily concerned about. Horrendous events may not score deeply in the heart at all, depending on God's grace. Slightest happenings may leave scars and resultant practices that wreck relationships from then on. What is important is the heart's reaction. Sometimes reactions are not apparent immediately, exploding later, much like a bomb with a delayed fuse.

Forgiveness concerning events may not yet accomplish deliverance. Reactions to events in childhood cause behavior adaptations, which become habits and practices in the flesh. Those behavior patterns, once firmly structured into the soul, are not easily dealt with. For example, we may react to coldness on the part of parents and build into ourselves the patterns of withdrawal, the stony heart, the habits of taking vengeance, and all the other writhing tentacles of the octopus of self. We should be more concerned about the practices in the flesh (Col. 3:9) than the events from which they are built. Just forgiving our parents will not set us free. We must also bring death through repentance to the consequent sinful practices.

We said earlier that if bad fruit persists, forgiveness is not yet accomplished. A person may, however, fully forgive the one who initially wounded and yet retain a destructive resulting practice. That practice is also dismantled (or transformed) by the cross—and forgiveness. When a person has forgiven another, he yet has himself to forgive. We cannot allow the destruction of our inner practices until forgiveness of self restores capacity to trust and to let go. Death of self is predicated upon and made possible only by the fullness of forgiveness. We cannot stand to be crucified with Him so long as we continue to blame and chastise ourselves and try to be different. Death of that striving to set things straight is built upon fullness of forgiveness, in which we cease to attack ourselves.

Forgiveness brings us to rest. The blood of Jesus washes away the strivings of guilt precisely so that the structures of habit can be let go to death. If you have prayed for the death of your sin and guilt on the cross many times, and yet that old pattern of sin continues to operate, there is a need to return to base one and examine whether fullness or forgiveness of self and God has in fact been accomplished.

The only route to the cross is through Gethsemane—which is when we identify our sin and wrestle our emotions away from attachment to the old way. Otherwise we will, in effect, snatch our old way off the cross before He cries out, "It is finished." Forgiveness happens *before* death, even as Jesus first petitioned, "Father, forgive them," hours before He was ready to proclaim once and for all, "It is finished." Fullness of forgiveness prepares us for happy, easy, deathlike letting go of a feather in a gentle wind. Without fullness of forgiveness, we put a practice on the cross, only to discover it still stuck on the hand, glued there by unforgiveness of self and God. Without fullness of forgiveness, the work of sanctification and transformation is heavy and sweaty. But forgiveness makes it light and easy.

TWO-PART TRANSFORMATION

Transformation has two parts. The blood of Jesus washes the heart clean, but the blood will not destroy the works of darkness in the soul (1 John 3:8). Only the cross can do that. Forgiveness is central, but it only begins the process. The work of transformation is a daily struggle from then on to crucify the self.

Some ongoing aspects of forgiveness can continue to influence and enhance that transformation. Pray that God will bless those who wounded or failed you (Rom. 12:14–21; 1 Pet. 3:8–14). Minister to others in like difficulties; as you do, you will see yourself more clearly, and love will overflow your own desert places.

Most especially, pray in thanksgiving for everything in the past. As you pray with thanksgiving, your heart will be changed from a stance of self-pity and anger to glorying in what God has accomplished in and through all.

Forgiveness is not complete until God the Father is included. Scripture says, "The foolishness of man subverts his way, and his heart rages against the LORD" (Prov. 19:3). Note again that word *heart*. The mind protests, "How could I ever be angry at God? He's so perfect. He never did anything to me." But that's not what the heart says. The heart perversely cries out, "Oh, yeah, if You were a good Father, You wouldn't have let me fall this far!" Or in the case of people wounded in early childhood, in the womb, or at birth, "You sent me to serve You, and then You let me get so messed up by these people. Now how do You expect me to serve You? It isn't fair!" Or, "Where were You when I needed You?" Or, "Why me, God?" And so on, the heart's cries being as infinite as the problems we get into.

For that reason Job cried out, "Neither is there any daysman betwixt us, that might lay his hand upon us both" (Job 9:33, KJV). A daysman was the same as a prayer minister in Bible times. Men went to such a man to settle disputes, as when the two women made King Solomon their daysman in their dispute over whose baby was whose (1 Kings 3:16–28). Such a prayer minister, or daysman, talked to both parties, reasoned with them, and, having settled the dispute, laid his hands on both their shoulders and drew them together for forgiveness. Job's cry calls for our Lord Jesus Christ to become our daysman betwixt God and man. And that is what 2 Corinthians 5:18–20 says He is, namely, that "God was in Christ reconciling the world to Himself." Observe in the last phrase of the quote, St. Paul speaks of our being reconciled to God, not the other way around. We need to be reconciled to God because we are angry with Him. In the next phrase the Holy Spirit speaks of His forgiving us: "not counting their trespasses against them." That is the function of the daysman, to lay his hand on each and so make mutual forgiveness and peace.

Jesus is our daysman. Through Him, we are to enable forgiveness between God and man, both ways.

CHAPTER 6

BREAKING the CYCLE

For as many as are of the works of the law are under the curse: for it is written, Cursed is every one that continueth not in all things which are written in the book of the law to do them. But that no man is justified by the law in the sight of God, it is evident: for, The just shall live by faith. And the law is not of faith: but, The man that doeth them shall live in them. Christ hath redeemed us from the curse of the law, being made a curse for us: for it is written, Cursed is every one that hangeth on a tree: That the blessing of Abraham might come on the Gentiles through Jesus Christ; that we might receive the promise of the Spirit through faith.

—GALATIANS 3:10–14, KJV

And they that are Christ's have crucified the flesh with the affections and lusts.

—GALATIANS 5:24, KJV

IT IS NOT ENOUGH merely to forgive. The existence of our undead flesh guarantees that we will repeat many of our offenses far more than four hundred ninety times (Matt. 18:21–22). If you will picture a prizefighter deftly warding off blows through countless rounds, defending against a relentless attacker, that may begin to portray the incessant need of forgiveness in a family so long as the flesh is not dealt with. Don't we all at times feel like martyrs who seem to have to do all the forgiving in the family and become dreadfully impatient for God to change everyone else? Habitual structures inflict so continually that they may eventually wear out the most patient saint. Therefore, the cross is central to survival. For Christ's blood washes away guilt for past hatreds. But only when we let it take us a step further, and die with Him on the cross is future hate prevented.

Repentance is not a *feeling*; it is *action*. It will not effect much change if we only feel sorry. Change happens in relationships solely as the cycle of hatred is broken and transformed by the stimuli of love. Change can happen in individuals, one by one, only in relationships. Change happens in individuals only as those structures that stimulate wrong actions and that respond to them are crucified on the cross. Without that crucifixion, battle scenes will be repeated in endlessly varied forms.

Many believers attempt to heal relationships by changing the surface ways people talk or act. Since all words and actions have behind them rivers of inner intention and hidden structures in the flesh, that is much like sticking a finger in a dike, only to discover another break and then another. Eventually one pictures a man splayed over a wall with every finger and toe engaged while emotions and incidents pour like a sieve all around him until the whole relationship bursts open.

By becoming as us in Gethsemane, our Lord Jesus Christ gained the right (necessitated by our free will) to die for us *as us* on the cross. That death crumbles the structures of self. The moment our physical body dies, the vacated spirit no longer has access to sustain its structures, and collapse and decay set in. The moment the attitude of our hearts finds its death knell on the cross, the structures it sustained begin to find their death on the cross. In each such successive inner death, we go through a process, one modeled for us by the forerunner and pioneer of our faith as He died and arose again. Like Jesus, after a while (three days in the belly of the earth), a new and resurrected spirit in us fills that old, newly dead structure with a new and transformed intention that can move through "locked doors and windows" (John 20:19–26) to meet and heal the hearts of others.

When death of a character structure happens, that portion of our inner being figuratively sinks "into the heart of the earth." "For just as Jonah was three days and three nights in the belly of the sea monster, so shall the Son of Man be three days and three nights in the heart of the earth" (Matt. 12:40). In biblical symbolism, the belly is the repository of thoughts and feelings. "He that believeth on me, as the scripture hath said, out of his belly[1] shall flow rivers of living water" (John 7:38, KJV).

Death of a portion of our self initiates a convulsion or deep shudder throughout our interior being. Such death is made sweet as the overwhelming presence of Jesus envelopes our hearts as we receive His healing touch. However, sometimes the opposite seems to occur, at least initially. When the heat of the Holy Spirit drives hidden dross to the surface of our hearts (Mal. 3:2), the purging can bring temporary discomfort. In such instances, we may undergo sadness, confusion, disorientation, despondency, heaviness, sleepiness, or turmoil. In that time, death is happening throughout the subterranean regions of our motives and practices. Truly we also, like Jesus, spend our three days in the belly of the earth.

The "three days" may be but a moment, or hours, days, or in rare cases weeks, depending on who knows what within the complexity of us. Paula and I have visited with many believers during their "three days." They may say any number of the following:

"I don't know what's happening to me."

"I'm so tired all the time."

"I feel so heavy I feel like I'm drugged."

" I don't seem to want to do anything."

"I don't seem to have my normal, usual feelings."

"I'm walking about like a zombie."

"I feel like a bowl of jelly inside."

"I'm all scrambled."

"I feel like an inner earthquake is rumbling around somewhere, and I can't get ahold of it."

"I just want to sleep all the time."

"You never told me it would be like this. How long does this go on? Is this normal?"

The most common experience is extremely heavy fatigue. Actually, what has happened is similar to what occurs in the first days of a much-needed vacation. When we let down, our fatigue catches up with us. The weariness is not actually new. It was there all along. Our letting down causes us to feel accumulated past fatigue in the present.

Jesus came to call the weary: "Come to Me, all who are weary and heavy-laden, and I will give you rest. Take My yoke upon you, and learn from Me, for I am gentle and humble in heart; and *you shall find rest for your souls.* For My yoke is easy, and My load is light" (Matt. 11:28–30, emphasis added). Every structure in the flesh is marked by unrest. Whatever in us that has been built by God is at rest, even as He rested (Heb. 4:10). Whatever we built in us has no rest; it must be constantly examined, reworked, defended, appreciated, and approved of. Thus, each practice demands energy to sustain itself. That is why sometimes our conscious mind forgets what it is doing. Our inner struggles rob the surface mind of its ability to concentrate by draining off its energy for more demanding inner battles. So when we come to death with Jesus on the cross, our inner being goes into the tomb with Him, and we let down into that emotional, mental, and spiritual fatigue that was there all along.

As we said earlier, however, such discomfort is the exception and not the rule. But we have lingered on the subject for the sake of those who may be experiencing such feelings and wonder what is happening to them.

In any case, that time of inner death cannot be hastened. Like Jesus, we need our "three days in the belly of the earth," however long or short that may be. We also need our Joseph of Arimathea and Nicodemus to be there as we come off the cross of death, to lay us lovingly to rest (Matt. 27:58–59). That means practically that we need people who can stand for us to change, people who are not threatened if we act differently or fail to act. People who stand by us, not forcing us to return to the old ways of acting. People who do nothing but stand there, accepting us, as we stop doing what is familiar to them. People who are not upset because we don't play the old games anymore. We need people who do not demand that we respond out of an erstwhile emotional center that is no longer there, who are not hurt, accusing, or controlling. People who let us be a dead mess and love us anyway.

We also need people like the Roman centurion and his soldiers, people who stand guard about us through the long night of our death. We cannot take the full clamor of new events and challenges during that time of inner death. We need people to pick up the slack for us, to handle details and not criticize when we flub a detail we used to do easily by rote. We need a pocket, like a quarterback depending on his guards to pick off the blitzers long enough for the play of life to unfold in a new way before us. There is an inner night of death we need to have time to go through.

We may not be ready quickly to be touched, like Jesus with Mary in the garden (John 20:17). As Jesus needed to go yet to His Father, so we may need quiet confirmations of the new life until it settles in, and "after you have suffered for a little, the God of all grace, who called you to His eternal glory in Christ, will Himself perfect, confirm, strengthen and establish you" (1 Pet. 5:10). And people may not recognize us (John 20:14; Luke 24:16). They are not used to the new us, and neither are we. So the old familiar demands upon us need to be held off for a while. Another analogy might be that we are like a newly overhauled motor that should not be run full bore until the new piston rings are well sealed. We need to ease into the new, old body of us. If hurried, we may not come into the fullness of rest and new identity we are meant to become.

ALLOW THE HIDDENNESS OF THE PROCESS

There is a hiddenness that ought to be respected. No one knows what happened to Jesus during those three days in the tomb. We know what He *did*: "For Christ also died for sins once for all, the just for the unjust, in order that He might bring us to God, having been put to death in the flesh, but made alive in the spirit; in which also He went and made proclamation to the spirits now in prison" (1 Pet. 3:18–19). But we do *not* know what kind of metamorphosis, if any, was happening to Him, or how. We know that He was made perfect through what He suffered (Heb. 2:10). Perhaps that perfection was continuing to be accomplished there, in the depths of suffering our death, unless "It is finished" referred as well to the process. Whether or not anything was continuing to happen *to* Jesus, it certainly does happen *in us* in our "three days in the belly of the earth." For that time, *introspection needs to stop.*

In prayer ministry, Paula and I have often felt the check of the Holy Spirit, prompting us to tell the person to quit "looking in" for that time period. The Lord at such times would reveal nothing further concerning the inner nature of the person to whom we were ministering and would make it apparent to us that this was not the time to deal with anything else already seen inside the person. Other things might later come to a time of death, but right then so much death and deep, hidden reformation was going on that we only wanted to sit and celebrate, seeing nothing further. We have often had to say to the person, "Will you quit digging up the seed to see how well it's doing and let well enough alone?" Our holy, spiritual advice then is to suggest the person read a mystery novel, watch a comedy program or movie, or play a game—anything to busy the mind outwardly—distracting it from interior speculations, so as to let the inner being alone.

How significant it is that Jesus came back into the same physically wounded body. Apart from all the theological significances, which could never be overstated, there lies an import to the inner being that is the essence of transformation. Our own new nature likewise arises within the very structure of what we have been. It is not that we would be OK if we could just get away from ourselves and move over there, somewhere else, and become some other personality. Maybe we would all like to be like that friend or neighbor whose character seems so ideal to us, or like some favorite saint. But God didn't call us to be like them. He called us to be us, and to become that new us within the very mess we have been, now transformed by the resurrection life of Jesus in us.

When Jesus restores us, He does not superimpose His own being in such a way that we are type-stamped, like cookie-cutter gingerbread creatures. Rather, His nature is still such a death of Himself for us that He fills out what we are to be, which is uniquely and gloriously us. We are not robbed of anything we have been by our own personal crucifixion. We are fulfilled. His life fills our life's structure with His resurrection power to be the glory He intended from the first that we should be: "There are also heavenly bodies and earthly bodies, but the glory of the heavenly is one, and the glory of the earthly is another. There is one glory of the sun, and another glory of the moon, and another glory of the stars; for star differs from star in glory. So also is the resurrection of the dead" (1 Cor. 15:40–42).

Our delightful God revels in variety. "How lovely are Thy dwelling places, O LORD of hosts!" (Ps. 84:1). "Or do you not know that your body is a temple of the Holy Spirit who is in you, whom you have from God, and that you are not your own?" (1 Cor. 6:19). "In whom you also are being built together into a dwelling of God in the Spirit" (Eph. 2:22). God will never turn out one individual like another. No one can be replaced. Every child of God is unique, glorious in his own right, and needful to the whole. Therefore, a prayer minister or lay leader does not build into another what the minister or leader thinks he ought to be. The greatest loss on earth would be a bunch of John and Paula Sandfords all acting identically. We fail if we produce clones. Every believer stands by to watch as Jesus resurrects another into that unique wonder of creation God intended for him/her to be. That is the joy of being called to be a minister: watching the unique beauty of each butterfly emerge.

As we said earlier, until inner death happens and the new creatures we are to be emerge, the cycle of hate is not broken. Our old habit patterns continue to incite trouble, both in others and us. And the battle is on again and again. Now we add that even if we are in process of catching the deceptive games of the self in some areas, in other areas we are but beginning or have not even started the labor of catching ourselves, checking our responses, and hauling them to the cross. There are no easy-to-come-by saints. There is only perseverance (Heb. 3:14; 12:1). Let but a momentary off-guardedness happen, and we are back into our outward battles. How tired of it we become. Peace does not fully come until we agree to allow the whole structure to be dealt with. Though full in the inmost spirit at the moment of *conversion*, peace does not settle into all our living until the entire inner being is submitted to the cross and the self is being transformed.

Even so, that transformation depends upon the continued grace of our Lord's presence in us. If we walk dry, apart from prayer, that arid condition becomes the ground of resurrection, not of the new but of the old. "Thou wilt keep him in perfect peace, whose mind is stayed on thee: because he trusteth in thee" (Isa. 26:3, KJV). Mark carefully, not that *we stay* the mind on Him by determination or whatever power of the flesh we could beckon to the task, but the mind "*is stayed*," is kept by the Lord. So the one who *abides* in Him bears much fruit (John 15:1–5). "And He was saying to them all, 'If anyone wishes to come after Me, let him deny himself, and take up *his cross daily,* and follow Me'" (Luke 9:23, emphasis added).

The most common factor we deal with in prayer ministry is the fact of undead flesh in born-anew Christians. Comprehension of crucifixion is crucial to the maturation of the body in Christ. Note, therefore, a difference: physical death is apt to be something easy and quick, but crucifixion is slow and painful. Evolvement is even slower and more painful. As there are no instant saints, neither are there sudden transformations.

Al Durance, an Episcopal rector friend of ours, likes to wear a T-shirt that reads, "The trouble with living sacrifices is, they keep crawling off the altar." How true! We may have to suffer the embarrassment of failures numbers of times and so deeply that we can't stand what we are more than we fear death—until we can't stand not dying to self.

We cannot very successfully put ourselves on the cross. We have to be impelled to it by the process He puts us through. If we could do it ourselves, we would never be able to escape the pride that we managed to become deader than the next fellow. "Well, my friend, you will be as holy as I am when you have just managed to die enough." The Lord so engineers our salvation that though we have a part in it, we can never take credit for our own crucifixion. In Christ all boasting is excluded: "That no man should boast before God. But by His doing you are in Christ Jesus, who became to us wisdom from God, and righteousness and sanctification, and redemption, that, just as it is written, '*Let him who boasts, boast in the Lord*'" (1 Cor. 1:29–31, emphasis added).

Only so does death and resurrection happen, by the providence of God. Now let us see whether every Christian can hear what follows from that fact: if it is the Holy Spirit who moves us by the grace of God's planning, at the right time and way, to our own personal crucifixion, what have we to do with judging any brother for being when and where he is? We are tempted to anger by the stubborn slowness, even tardiness, of others and us, but when we come to understand the way we all must come to crucifixion solely by His timing, all hustle and demand die. For we see that God in His wisdom knows how to move us on the checkerboard of life. Can we blame a brother for being immature? Had God not persisted, despite our stubbornness, there we would be also. Maybe it is not that fellow's time yet. Let it be only God who judges whether he is tardy and rebellious or not.

"Truly, truly, I say to you, when you were younger, you used to gird yourself, and walk wherever you wished; but when you grow old, you will stretch out your hands, and someone else will gird you, and bring you where you do not wish to go" (John 21:18). When Jesus spoke to Peter, He referred specifically to the time when men would carry Peter to be crucified upside down. But notice, the context is crucifixion, and the text can be taken as a parable for us. When we were first born anew and filled with the Spirit, we steamed ourselves up (girded ourselves) in our emotions and by our individual prayer life. We rushed here and there, sharing this word and that, trying this and that gift, to get our own ministry going. We "went where we would." Maturity in Jesus means crucifixion, the point being that He accomplishes that crucifixion through the means of where others *take us.* We "put forth our hands," both to minister and to be ministered to. But others take hold of us and carry us where we would not—to death of self.

We need to be encouraging others to stop fighting the people and circumstances God puts in our way. It may be those very incidents and people who carry us to our death (which is most likely precisely why we *do* fight them). We may not be able to stop fighting. We may not like the whole process. But at least we understand it. And praise God for it (with gritted teeth, perhaps): "Though he slay me, yet will I trust in him" (Job 13:15, KJV). We assert so often, "He is Lord." Do we really mean it? Or believe it? Does the unbelieving heart of a believer actually expect that His lordship means that He *will* put us through the process? Perhaps we can learn nothing more valuable in all of life than to trust that He really is who He is and will accomplish what He has purposed to do, "that He might present to Himself the church in all her glory, having no spot or wrinkle or any such thing; but that we should be holy and blameless" (Eph. 5:27). "Now to Him who is able to keep you from stumbling, and to make you stand in the presence of His glory blameless with great joy..." (Jude 24).

HANG ON TO YOUR HEALING

We cannot close this chapter without teaching how to keep one's healing. There is a necessity to stand on faith. Once crucifixion is in process, or being completed, we need to claim that fact by what we allow ourselves to feel, think, say, or do. We need to continue to reckon as dead that thing we prayed about. Many people go directly from healing prayer to a testing, and, feeling that same old emotion, they conclude, "Oh, it didn't work." They may then plunge right back into all the same old feelings. Old habits will continue to sound off, like chime stones swinging in the wind. But if we have taken a thing to the cross, that is all they are, mere sounds in the wind, having no force of reality behind them anymore. They are truly dead, and we are made new. But if we believe they still have life and plunge into struggling with them, we impart false life to those old crucified structures and wrestle unnecessarily all over again.

A habit of jealousy or temper or being critical—whatever—will keep on flaring up, having been prayed for. But if we have laid the ax to the root and prayed, that thing is, in fact, dead. If we let the continued recurrence of the old habit bother us, we can be stampeded only by ghosts and old, empty, haunted houses in our character. It is often merely because of that fact of unbelief, and lack of self-discipline, that believers fall back until "the last state has become worse for them than the first" (2 Pet. 2:20).

If a believer struggling toward transformation believes that old thing still has reality, he will either give it energy by grappling with it or give in and flop back into the old habit. Neither is necessary. All he has to do is reject the old feeling, not fighting with it, merely saying, "I don't have to have that anymore. That is dead," and then go on with the life he wants, ignoring contrary feelings from that point on. Or if it's a thought or an action, he needs only to reject the old thought or deed, from that point on ignoring that thought and making himself act in a new way, without bothering to question or quarrel with himself or even concern himself that that old thing still exists. Thus he gives it no reality.

The old form in the flesh, once dealt with, can be likened to a swinging pendulum in a grandfather clock, the main spring of which is broken. If we will let it alone and not hit the pendulum again, pretty soon it will wind down and quit. Or as with a bouncing ball, if we will quit dribbling it, it will eventually stop bouncing and roll to a stop. We must learn not to pay attention to dead symptoms. All our feelings have a life of their own, and they do not want to die. Our thoughts likewise fight not to perish. If we get in and fight with them again, the feelings and thoughts will have a grand time plunging us into problem after problem just to keep themselves alive and on center stage.

> Therefore do not *let* sin reign in your mortal body that you should obey its lusts, and do not go on presenting the members of your body to sin as instruments of unrighteousness; but present yourselves to God as those alive from the dead, and your members as instruments of righteousness to God. For sin

shall not be master over you, for you are not under law, but under grace.

—ROMANS 6:12–14, EMPHASIS ADDED

Our minds and hearts do not want us to be whole. They want to cook up crisis after crisis. "Because the mind set on the flesh is hostile toward God; for it does not subject itself to the law of God, for it is not even able to do so" (Rom. 8:7). We haul such habits of mind and heart *daily* to death after prayer by acting the new life and ignoring the old signals.

A woman came who could not give herself to her husband sexually. After we found the roots and brought all the old self-structures to the cross, she still found herself tensing at her husband's approach. Her mind and feelings ran scattered like rebellious children. She learned not to fight her feelings or her mind or get mad at her continued failures. Rather, she said silently, "I reject that," and turned her attention to receiving her husband's touch and spirit. She was soon warm and loving and having a ball, and so was he.

A woman came oppressed by feelings of worthlessness, loneliness, and self-pity. Having gotten at the roots, she had to learn not to let herself be tyrannized by continued recurrence of the old feelings, and she made herself do things that distracted her mind from the symptoms. In a few weeks she couldn't remember what she used to feel.

A man came who could not spend time with his children and enjoy it. The roots being taken care of, he found that the new life he desired was no automatic gift. He had to take hold and make himself be with his children, play games, take walks, go fishing, and read stories to them, ignoring the pull of TV and all the old feelings and non-feelings. After a while he was having so much fun with his children he wondered why he never had discovered such joy before.

A final point. We have found it to be a law that those who merely want pain removed do not get well. Those who want to go on enjoying their own selfish, self-centered life never become free and happy. They only want to escape trouble (the very thing God would use to wake them up) so they can go on serving their own selfish god of mammon pleasure. But those whose joy it is to lay their lives down in service for others are soon well and happy. The secret of life is, in fact, to lose it (Luke 17:33).

CHAPTER 7

THE ROLE OF A PRAYER MINISTER

Before she travailed, she brought forth;
Before her pain came, she gave birth to a boy.
Who has heard such a thing? Who has seen such things?
Can a land be born in one day?
Can a nation be brought forth all at once?
As soon as Zion travailed, she also brought forth her sons.
"Shall I bring to the point of birth, and not give delivery?" says
    the LORD.
"Or shall I who gives delivery shut the womb?" says your God.
"Be joyful with Jerusalem and rejoice for her, all you who love
    her;
Be exceedingly glad with her, all you who mourn over her;
That you may nurse and be satisfied with her comforting
    breasts;
That you may suck and be delighted with her bountiful
    bosom."
For thus says the LORD, "Behold, I extend peace to her like a
    river,
And the glory of the nations like an overflowing stream;

And you shall be nursed, you shall be carried on the hip and
    fondled on the knees.
As one whom his mother comforts, so I will comfort you;
And you shall be comforted in Jerusalem."

                        —Isaiah 66:7–13

God intends to give daily rebirth and nurture to us through the Church. The Church is now called to give birth anew, more and more, to the Church. That, we believe, is the primary calling upon the body of Christ today.

"And do not be conformed to this world, but be transformed by the renewing of your mind, that you may prove what the will of God is, that which is good and acceptable and perfect" (Rom. 12:2). Note the little word *by*. We have wondered why sometimes we are simply healed by the Lord and why at other times it seems we must obtain just the right bit of knowledge in order to be sanctified in a given area. Some have made such an issue of *mental* comprehension and confession for people to come into fullness of redemption and maturity that it seems to us they have enthroned the conscious mind!

To be transformed *by* the renewal of the mind does not mean that we must all become auto-analysts, excavating every moment of our history into the light (or confusion) of mental awareness. Some things may be better left unseen and unsaid. Sometimes the Lord renews our deep mind without our ever having consciously understood. We simply find ourselves thinking differently, for "out of the heart come evil thoughts" (Matt. 15:19). If the *heart* is changed by the Lord, the mind, both conscious and subconscious, *is renewed.* Sometimes we simply grow out of a childish way. We have thought as children and reasoned so, but when we became adults in Christ, we put that away (1 Cor. 13:11).

Many prayer ministers have erred by driving the person receiving ministry to see and examine everything, as though we are saved by right thinking. That is gnosticism. Rather, we are saved by the person of our Lord Jesus Christ, and both the person ministering and the one receiving ministry alike must be open to His Holy Spirit to see only what *He* knows is pertinent to our transformation.

For the transformation that goes on without our conscious awareness, the general body of Christ is easily both our womb and our midwife. But for those instances in which the Holy Spirit requires that we understand ourselves, the priesthood of all believers may or may not be sufficient. Those who are our compatriots in Christ should be our first prayer ministers. Sometimes, however, a person of special insight is needed. "A plan ["purposes" in NIV] in the heart of a man is like deep water, but a man of understanding draws it out" (Prov. 20:5).

The scriptural base for every minister in Christ is found in what Jesus was and is as expressed in Isaiah 11:1–3:

> Then a shoot will spring up from the stem of Jesse,
> And a branch from his roots will bear fruit.
> And the Spirit of the Lord will rest on Him,
> The spirit of wisdom and understanding,
> The spirit of counsel and strength,
> The spirit of knowledge and the fear of the Lord.
> And He will delight in the fear of the Lord,
> And He will not judge by what His eyes see,
> Nor make a decision by what His ears hear.

A prayer minister must not judge by what his eyes see or his ears hear. He must see beyond events and circumstances with the gift of insight. A prayer minister must look, as God does, upon the heart. "For God sees not as man sees, for man looks at the outward appearance, but the LORD looks at the heart" (1 Sam. 16:7). Sight alone endangers the beholder with judgment. "Do not judge lest you be judged. For in the way you judge, you will be judged; and by your standard of measure, it shall be measured to you" (Matt. 7:1–2). It is not that we must never judge. We cannot live without making appraisals and acting accordingly. We judge whether a bridge is safe to cross, whether a piece of merchandise is worth its cost, or whether we ought to entrust our life to a particular doctor's skill. More pertinently, we decide whether we ought to risk our confidences with a man or trust our emotions with his temperament or our confessions to his confidentiality or to his concepts of authority and forgiveness.

It is the stance of the heart that matters. The above Scripture passage concerns blaming and condemning. Christian ministers must hold firm the knowledge that in Christ there is no condemnation (Rom. 8:1). We stand together at the foot of the cross, seeing we are all under sin. No one is better than another, however well some may have performed. Otherwise, seeing another's fault, we become self-elevated. A minister sees and judges, but never with blame. He attempts to see not the surface but the intent of the heart, and so judges not the *context* but the true *content* of what is happening.

"Woe is me, for I am ruined! Because I am a man of unclean lips, *and I live among a people of unclean lips*" (Isa. 6:5, emphasis added). A prayer minister must consider his brother's sin as his own. It is of no consequence that we dwell *among* sinners unless we know their sins as ours. We are one, whether we want it so or not. The fact that a prayer minister may not have succumbed to that particular sin is not to his credit, but to the Lord's grace. If he does not know these things, he cannot help but feel himself better than the one to whom he ministers.

Further, to the extent that a prayer minister thinks the blood has washed him lily white, remaining unaware that his flesh yet runs rampant, his ministry will also put down rather than set free. He will look down on those to whom he ministers. Every ministry (preaching, teaching, and evangelism) stands in danger of this, but it is most likely to happen in the close confines of the prayer ministry office. Prayer ministers more than all others wade the sewers of human hearts. If a minister does not know he belongs there (in the sewer) and deserves no better than any life he sees, he cannot help but become puffed up like the Pharisee and send not only himself but also the person receiving ministry home unjustified (Luke 18:9–14). Such a minister may try to appear understanding, but he will come across as condescending, for the person will sooner or later read his heart. If a minister cannot see himself to be as rotten as any other sinner, accepting himself as finite and broken, he cannot bring another into rest or give Jesus all the glory. He will scold and scald, or he will palliate sin and whitewash walls (Ezek. 13:10–15). To know himself as sinful is the *sine qua non* qualification of every prayer minister in the Lord Jesus Christ!

> Is anyone among you sick? Let him call for the elders of the church, and let them pray over him, anointing him with oil in the name of the Lord; and the prayer offered in faith will restore the one who is sick, and the Lord will raise him up, and if he has committed sins, they will be forgiven him. Therefore, confess your sins to one another, and pray for one another, so that you may be healed. The effective prayer of a righteous man can accomplish much.
>
> —James 5:14–16

> Iron sharpens iron, so one man sharpens another.
>
> —Proverbs 27:17

> Where there is no guidance, the people fall, but in abundance of counselors there is victory.
>
> —Proverbs 11:14

In the beginning when people sat down in front of me (John) for prayer ministry, fright would threaten to undo me. I felt like I had to perfect them, all at once—and who was I to do that? Wisdom soon revealed that was not my task, only to do the thing the Holy Spirit prompted that day. But the fear assailed in another direction. How was I to know what was needful just then? That fear is long overcome but still residual. Each time you find that God has placed you in the role of ministering to another believer, the prayer that should ascend from your heart is this: "Lord, make me appropriate to where he is. Cause me to catch the clues. Make me sensitive to what You are doing in the other. Give me wisdom to help, not to interfere or throw off the track."

Unlike a psychological counselor, a prayer minister most likely will not use psychological tests to discover what is in the other. He must rely on the Holy Spirit to reveal the details to be dealt with on a particular day. Whatever is seen is not viewed as the problem to be attacked and overcome but as the context for the Holy Spirit to "perfect, confirm, strengthen and establish" (1 Pet. 5:10).

MINISTRY MODELS

Consequently, a prayer minister can be described by several models. First, he is a father-confessor, as in James 5:16. Hearing the confession of another, he probes for causes, admonishes and teaches as a father, and expresses forgiveness as a part of his priesthood in the priesthood of all believers.

Second, he is a shepherd, pouring on oil and providing still water. The thick wool of sheep prevents ticks from attaching to all parts of the body except the face and ears. A shepherd carefully examines each sheep each night, and if a tick is found, pours on oil until the tick backs out. "A tick of the mind" is an oriental idiom to describe a way of thinking that drains energy that "sucks the blood of life," such as hate, vengeance, or resentment. The oil is, of course, the Holy Spirit's anointing.

Sheep cannot drink fast water. It will bloat them. They must have still water. If he cannot find naturally still water, the shepherd digs a small hole by a stream and then a channel to it. Fast waters are the racing and troubled thoughts and emotions of the soul. The shepherd-minister becomes a quiet and calm pool of listening, acceptance, and counsel.

Third, a minister is a midwife. People frequently dream of struggling to give birth or not to miscarry or some other such birth or baby dream or nightmare. By that our inner being is portraying to the surface mind an inner trauma of something being born in us— a new idea, a realization, a new talent, or, on the other side, some evil thought or resurrection of the flesh. Some such births need to happen; some need to be prevented. A minister is sometimes called on to be the Lord's midwife, to assist the other in the birth process.

Fourth, he is also an executioner, slaying the little monsters born of sinful wombs of the mind, heart, and soul. He assists the other to the cross and helps him to hold himself there until the job is done.

Fifth, he is a spiritual director, one who hears the whole life and calls for balance or helps to set direction and pace. He may say, "You've been working at it too hard. It would be a good idea to take your wife out to dinner and a show." Or, "Try reading this (or that)." Or, "Have you considered praying this way?" Or, "Don't read so much for a while." He suggests whatever he sees is the needed next step in the person's life or whichever counterbalancing thing needs to be done.

Finally, he may become as a father or mother in Christ.

A prayer minister is a friend who ministers. He is not merely a Christian who happens to counsel. Every Christian occasionally counsels and should improve his skills. People have come to us wounded and in increased confusion because they have been advised by many and ministered to by some, sincere in their desire to help but untrained and unskilled. Too often the one who ministers tends to project his own experience or problems onto the one to whom he ministers, whether it fits him or not. A prayer minister must call his own knowledge and experience to death on the cross daily so that he may be appropriate to the person, fresh and open to him and to the Holy Spirit. That requires a learned discipline. Our hope is to be a part of that training of the entire body of Christ to minister. But some in the body are especially called to prayer ministry. Often when we speak of prayer ministers or lay leaders in this book, we have in mind those Christians who have been distinctly called, gifted by the Holy Spirit to minister, and who hopefully are being recognized, called, and anointed by their pastors and churches.

There are psychologically trained counselors who happen to be Christian and counsel as such. Though our material may be helpful to them, we write primarily to prayer ministers within the body of Christ. We want to make it as clear as possible that we do not reject all psychology and psychological counseling. Although the philosophical foundations of psychology contain some serious flaws, much of the data learned through the field can be quite useful. We treasure truths others have discovered by observing God's creation. But we do not counsel as psychologists. We counsel as Christians, according to the Word of God. In that context, psychological perceptions are helpful if they support scriptural principles.

Occasionally an unbeliever may come for ministry. We are as straightforward as we can be, saying, "We minister as Christians. Our method and only power are the cross and prayer. If you can accept that, we'll be glad to help, but if not, you are free to find someone else." We may go on to include that while we will not demand that the person accept Jesus as Lord and Savior, nor even ask that he have faith (Luke 5:20–24), we will not be restrained in ministering by faith, and he needs to know and accept that. Somewhere in the ministry process, the person usually receives Jesus as his Lord and Savior.

We do not believe in prayer for the inner transformation of someone with whom we have not ministered to or who is not present with us. The inner regions of another are holy and private ground. We have no right there, except by verbal, present invitation. Some time ago a teacher in the body of Christ began to instruct people to pray for others while they were asleep, asking God to change them. We regard that as reprehensible. That is unfair, a manipulation of the other, bordering on magic. Though God has all power, He never changes anyone in such a way as to violate the person's free will.

We make two exceptions. Parents are ordained of God to raise children, thus to form their character. Children before teenage years can be prayed for concerning the inner man by their parents while the children are asleep. A couple came concerned for their little boy, who could not stop wetting the bed. We instructed them to go into his room after he had fallen asleep and pray affirmative prayers softly aloud, giving thanks for their son, filling him with love. They did, and within a week he had stopped bed-wetting. We did not instruct them to pray about or mention the bed-wetting problem, only to pray affirmative prayers of love for the inner child.

My (John's) cousin was given up by psychiatrists as a hopeless cause. She was to be confined to an asylum for the rest of her life. That is the second exception. Such a person does not have the fullness of her own mind or willpower. Nevertheless we regarded her inner being as holy ground. We prayed for the healing of the inner man, apart from her, without telling her or my uncle about it. Within a few weeks she was rediagnosed as totally well and was released. Today she has a husband and children and a perfectly normal life. We have never told her that we prayed, especially not what or how. Nor would we have prayed at all had not the Holy Spirit called and commanded. (We can imagine Christians, having read this, trying to empty asylums by prayer—wearing themselves out to little avail!)

Body Ministry in the Local Church

We believe that body ministry should be happening regularly in every church, especially in small groups. As that happens, there will be instances in which the small group feels that the expertise of someone especially gifted to minister to a particular individual is needed. Such persons could then be sent within the body to lay ministers who are recognized by pastors and elders. In the church in Spokane, that is what we had in operation. Prayer ministers worked with those sent by the groups and then returned them to their groups for support and continued ministry. Sometimes what could be reported without breaking confidence was told to the leaders of the groups to help them continue to minister.

Pastors may counsel, but it is our experience that pastors cannot carry a full counseling load and continue to shepherd the entire flock. One of the most compelling reasons we write this book is to say to pastors and churches the counsel of Jethro to Moses:

> The thing that you are doing is not good [counseling from morning until evening]. You will surely wear out, both yourself and these people who are with you, for the task is too heavy for you; you cannot do it alone. Now listen to me: *I shall give you counsel,* and God be with you. You be the people's representative before God, and you bring the disputes to God, then *teach them* the statutes and the laws, and make known to them the way in which they are to walk, and the work they are to do. Furthermore, *you shall select* out of all the people *able men who fear God, men of truth, those who hate dishonest gain;* and you shall place these over them, as leaders of thousands, of hundreds, of fifties and of tens. And *let them judge the people at all times;* and let it be that every *major* dispute they will bring to you, but every *minor* dispute they themselves will judge. So it will be easier for you, and *they will bear the burden with you.* If you do this thing and God so commands you, then *you will be able to endure,* and all these people also *will go to their place in peace.*
>
> —EXODUS 18:17–23, EMPHASIS ADDED

It needs to be remembered that Moses was the leader of a church-state. There was no separation of church and state. Moses was actually sitting as a magistrate over a civil court, settling civil disputes in the public body. From Jethro's counsel to Moses, our entire jurisprudence system has grown.

Nevertheless, the same counsel pertains to all pastors. Pastors cannot settle all the affairs of the heart of all the members of their churches, not even in a church as small as one hundred members. No pastor can have that much time and energy. Therefore elders who can shepherd and care for the sheep of the congregations should be raised up.

Some prayer ministers may have to overcome unscriptural, off-balance childhood teachings concerning confession. When Paula and I grew up, our arm of Protestantism was overreacting to what was regarded as abuses of the confessional in the Roman Catholic Church. We heard many false teachings, such as, "One should never confess his sins to another human being, only to God." "Confess your sins in secret to God only; He will hear in secret and reward you openly." Nowhere in the Bible is there a commandment to confess sins in secret! The one reference to praying in secret is in Matthew 6:6: "But you, when you pray, go into your inner room, and when you have shut the door, pray to your Father who is in secret, and your Father who sees in secret will repay you." The context has to do with personal piety and almsgiving (v. 4), not confession of sins. Jesus repeated His admonition to pray in secret in relation to fasting (v. 18). But none of that was a command to confess our sins privately. Rather, the command is to "confess your sins to *one another*" (James 5:16, emphasis added).

Consequently, many elders and prayer ministers have felt unnecessarily awkward or out of place expressing God's forgiveness. Praise God that He is rediscovering to us today that expressing forgiveness is not only ours to do, but also it is the *first* gift connected with reception of the Holy Spirit! "And when He had said this, He breathed on them, and said to them, 'Receive the Holy Spirit. If you forgive the sins of any, their sins have been forgiven them; if you retain the sins of any, they have been retained'" (John 20:22–23). By giving authority to forgive sins immediately upon breathing the Holy Spirit upon them, Jesus was saying that the very first consequence of having the Holy Spirit is authority to forgive sins! One might object that by forgiving sins we supplant the one true "mediator…between God and men, the man Christ Jesus" (1 Tim. 2:5). Not so, if that mediator Himself has commissioned us. By His decree, we act as ambassadors, acting not in our own authority, but under His auspices, in His name.

By placing these together, Jesus was saying that the power to forgive the sins of others in Jesus' name is the natural birthright and position of every Holy Spirit–filled son of God! He was also thereby making a powerful statement of importance, as though the forgiving of sins is the first and most-needed work of every normal Christian. Notice also that authority to forgive sins was given before any other manifestation of the presence of the Holy Spirit! Not until ten days later did the power of the Holy Spirit descend. It is as though Jesus wanted the disciples to know that ability to pronounce forgiveness is in no way dependent on power (*dunamis*) but solely on authority (*exousia*). They were to forgive sins before they had any power in the Holy Spirit! Perhaps also this gift had to be given immediately, before Pentecost, because in those ten days the one hundred twenty would need to confess their sins one to another and pronounce forgiveness for one another in preparation for fullness to descend on Pentecost!

It is still so today. It is as though the Church has been breathed on but is not living in the fullness. We have not yet come to Pentecost, thinking the first signs were the fullness. But few yet can walk up to a man lame *from birth* and say, "I do not possess silver and gold, but what I do have I give to you: In the name of Jesus Christ the Nazarene—walk!" (Acts 3:6). Notice Peter's use of the personal pronoun "I." *I* possess. *I* give. Miracles do happen today. We have the first breathing of the Spirit. But who among us has the audacity to *command, knowing* the miracle *will* happen right then as we say and expect? Who among us has the humility to say, "What *I* do have *I* give?" Kathryn Kuhlman and others can call out when and where God is working a miracle, but that is by description, not by personal command, knowing beyond all doubt it will happen as Peter knew.

As you see, we do not have the fullness of Pentecost. We maintain that perhaps the primary reason the fullness has not come is because we have not spent our ten days confessing to one another our sins! We heard the word *tarry*, and some have fasted and prayed long—*individually*. But "church" has not yet happened. We are not yet corporate. We have been too falsely taught, too frightened of vulnerability, too unwilling to be open, honest, and real. Pentecost happened when "all were together in one place" (Acts 2:1). We aren't together yet, even if geographically in the same room. It is the task of prayer ministers to hear confession in order to get the body of Christ into one place, that Pentecost may truly happen.

Whoever hears a confession should pronounce forgiveness in the first person: "In the name of Lord Jesus Christ, according to His Word, *I* pronounce that you are forgiven your sin of ___. As far as the east is from the west, so far..." It is not as effective merely to say, "Your sins are forgiven in Jesus' name," or "The Bible says you are forgiven." Many Protestants might reject this concept outright, simply because it sounds too "Catholic." Some object on the basis of 1 Timothy 2:5: "For there is one God, and one mediator also between God and men, the man Christ Jesus." But what such persons (and even some Catholics) do not understand is that even Catholic theology teaches that the priest confessor must not, in fact, replace Christ as mediator between God and men. According to the catechism, "Only God forgives sins." The priest can forgive only "in His name." Christ is the true mediator; the priest must work under Christ's auspices. At the same time, he mediates between the church and men, pronouncing forgiveness on behalf of the church for whatever way one's sin has wounded his brothers.[1]

We would not advocate anything that would oppose the principle laid down in 1 Timothy 2:5. Nor would Jesus. He Himself has given us the power to forgive as ambassadors of the one true mediator. And the idea that we can mediate between men and the church is entirely in keeping with Scripture. For when a man sins, that sin denigrates mankind. When Achan sinned, all Israel lost power (Josh. 7). When David sinned, his son died (2 Sam. 12:13–14). If one member *sins*, all suffer. Whenever we hear a confession, we have been placed in a position to represent mankind. Mankind has been injured; mankind needs to forgive. Our saying, "*I* forgive you" is essential to accomplish forgiveness from man. "In Jesus' name" effects forgiveness from God and heaven. We need to pronounce the forgiveness in several ways, repetitively, until the inner being is fully comforted and assured.

In Christianity's earliest days, confessions were heard by the entire church body. But because of the immaturity of some and the ever-present chance of gossip, priests were soon commissioned to hear confessions and pronounce forgiveness on behalf of the church. As Protestants, Paula and I believe that as members of the priesthood of all believers (1 Pet. 2:5), any mature and confidential believer is able to hear confessions and pronounce forgiveness. However, we choose to show proper respect toward our Catholic brothers. According to their faith, any Christian can hear what their church calls a "therapeutic confession," but only a priest can pronounce absolution. When we Protestants minister to Catholics, there can be no harm in deferring to their priest as the one who pronounces absolution. But it would be disrespectful and divisive to usurp our brother's place.

Years ago, Sister Linda Koontz took me to Bishop Topal of the Spokane Diocese to ask permission for me as a Protestant pastor to be spiritual director for nuns in his diocese. He asked me one question: "What would you do if one of my nuns made a confession to you?" I personally believe that I can pronounce forgiveness in Jesus' name for anyone, but I knew that deferring to his practice did not in any way deny my own moral stance; it only showed respect for my brother's right to choose. The Word commands, "Be devoted to one another in brotherly love; give preference to one another in honor" (Rom. 12:10). Therefore I replied, "I would send her to a priest for absolution." The bishop responded, "In that case, you can be spiritual director for nuns in my diocese."

Whatever one believes about who should pronounce forgiveness, hearing of confessions one to another is vital because the foundation stone of Christian transformation is the cross of Christ! Apart from the cross, there can be no Christian healing or transformation. Every minister must know that indelibly and irrevocably. That means our primary method is always prayer, the route always repentance and forgiveness. Having heard of a violent father, for example, we fail to transform if we only comfort. By such "healing" alone, the victim is left able to "throw a pity party." Nothing is resolved. The person feels only momentarily relieved because someone has heard him and buttressed his self-excusing stances. In actuality, the minister has thrown water on a fire God was building and thereby postponed confession of anger and bitterness. The person to whom he ministers may feel falsely justified and, most assuredly, will continue his patterns of retaliation, whether by aggression or withdrawal.

Nothing can defile us from outside. Only what comes out of our hearts can defile (Mark 7:15–21). Therefore, we are always dealing not so much with what was done to us as with our sinful responses. Reactions of resentment and judgment, however hidden and forgotten in the heart, must find their way to the cross, or guilt remains—with all its appendages. Habitual patterns of response must be transformed by repentance, death, and rebirth. Otherwise, no permanent or even valuable change of personality or behavior will result.

Every believer desiring transformation in the hidden recesses of the heart must know and see that sanctification is the work of the

Holy Spirit, and only His. He moves upon us in His own mysterious ways, within the Father's timetable. His plan is the Father's. His actions are totally in tune with the Father's perfect will for us.

Hypnotism in counseling involves not only occultic error, but it may also release power to demonic and/or fleshly forces to discover what the Holy Spirit would not yet or perhaps ever reveal (so, by the way, may many methods in counseling, unless we submit them to the check of the Holy Spirit; such is the Lord's ability to risk His work with us faulty workmen!). No Christian counselor or lay minister should be involved with hypnotism: "Let no one be found among you who sacrifices his son or daughter in the fire, who practices divination or sorcery, interprets omens, engages in witchcraft, *or casts spells,* or who is a medium, or spiritist or who consults the dead" (Deut. 18:10–11, NIV, emphasis added). If he needs to know what is hidden, let him use the gifts of insight in the Holy Spirit, not forbidden resources of the flesh.

However psychological his training, however informed his mind, a Christian counselor remains, as we have said earlier, a midwife, assisting the Holy Spirit and the other person in the arena of birth. He must not draw forth by force or too soon, nor should he fail to catch the idea that plops from the deep womb of thought. The minister is not the initiator of what happens, nor is he the controller. He catches the vision of what God is doing in the other, and celebrates and assists. He is not passive. All his energies are bent to identify with both God and man, to empathize with both the Holy Spirit and the person, so as to sense wherein and how the Holy Spirit is moving upon the man and what is rising in the person. He is not using psychological models to try to analyze. He is restfully active in the gift of insight, a coach upon the sidelines (Isa. 11:2).

Because the Holy Spirit leads, the person to whom we minister is the responder. Some schools of thought, such as Rogerian counseling, teach that the counselor should not interrupt or distract the counselee from what the individual's inner psyche brings forth. That stance grants the initiative to the flesh rather than the Spirit. The kernel of truth for the prayer minister or lay leader is that he ought not to detract from what the Holy Spirit is bringing to light. The minister's task is to direct the individual continually to the whispering of the Spirit's truth in his ear. In short, a prayer minister or lay leader helps the other to understand how the Holy Spirit is working in his life and how to respond in repentance, confession, action, or whatever the Holy Spirit prompts.

The Holy Spirit is working, in myriads of countless details, in every life to inform, teach, prepare, please, enthuse, enjoy, convict, worship—whatever enhances fellowship with God and man, whatever sanctifies and matures in faith. The minister's task is not to orchestrate all that work, and thus usurp God's position, but to be attentive to that move of the Holy Spirit of which God in that moment would have the minister be aware. Perhaps the minister cannot help but see many patterns of deceit or talents that need to be encouraged. He is not called to act by that seeing. He opens only that can of worms the Holy Spirit prompts, or affirms when He says to.

It is not enough to see what the Holy Spirit is doing or what He would reveal to the person receiving ministry; the call for wisdom is to learn what part the Holy Spirit would have the prayer minister or lay leader play. Should he blurt out an insight? Ask a question? Pose a parable or a riddle? Tell a story? Or set a trap, as Nathan caused David to judge his own case (2 Sam. 12:1–14)?

The problem usually is not the difficulty of seeing, nor is it to cause the other's *mind* to comprehend, but so to assist the process of discovery so that the Holy Spirit can write understanding *in the heart.* For that difficulty, St. Paul prayed that "the *eyes of [the] heart* may be enlightened" (Eph. 1:18, emphasis added) and for the inner man to be strengthened with might through faith that "[he] may have power to comprehend" (Eph. 3:18, paraphrased).

Prayer ministers must be restrained by the knowledge that it is the Holy Spirit who sanctifies by leading us out of old ways into *the* Way. As was said earlier, sometimes He cleanses and purifies without our ever knowing or needing to know what was wrong. The temptation upon the minister is to do too much or to hurry the process. It is the Lord who permeates us with His death as our death and raises us to resurrection life. But since the minister empathizes in the process and has been there many times both for himself and others, he may assume too glibly that the other comprehends, or he may leap too quickly to the denouement (successful conclusion). If he does, then like a hasty ferryboat captain, he may discover to his chagrin much of his cargo still on the dock! Or he may encourage the person too much to try and thus throw him into the common error of psychological counseling—Pelagianism—"You can do it," or "I can lift myself by my own bootstraps," or "I can see and change my own character." Pelagianism is the trap of self-striving, doomed to failure in the end. Only Jesus will bring to birth and not fail to bring forth (Isa. 66:9–11). Only He will not fail to present us without spot or wrinkle before the Father (Eph. 5:27). In that fact is our rest, for the prayer minister and the person receiving ministry alike. We don't have to make the other grow up (or ourselves). It is God who will sanctify us wholly—spirit, soul, and body (1 Thess. 5:23).

That is the *primary* difference between psychological counseling and Christian ministry. Often both may see the same thing. The secular psychologist waits for something to happen in the other, once seen and understood. His faith is in the power of the other's flesh to change. The minister, whether he is psychologically trained or a beginning layman, stands and watches as Christ delivers and transforms by the power of the cross.

Countless times men and women have come to us saying, "I have been going for six years (or so) to psychiatrists. I know all my hang-ups and why I have them. And I still have them!" Again, this is not meant to criticize psychologists, psychiatrists, or professional mental health counselors; a prayer minister may be both. It is to say again that for all who minister as Christians, our base is not psychology, either in hearing or acting for the person. Our power is the cross and the Spirit. We have the answer that works. Let's use it.

Ministers should also remember that although sanctification is the work of the Holy Spirit in us, needing only the continual response of a person's willingness, it is not so with transformation. Transformation requires more than willingness. Sanctification is largely *done to us.* Transformation involves *our* more active *participation* as He accomplishes the work *in us.* Transformation is effected by the "renewing of your mind" (Rom. 12:2). Since, as we have said, renewal of the mind comprises more than conscious mentality and the mind, surface and deep, must ponder, we have a larger part in the struggle. "I buffet my body" (1 Cor. 9:27). "I [myself, of my own discipline in Him] count all things…[as] but rubbish" (Phil. 3:8). "The carnal mind is enmity against God [therefore requiring personal struggle to bring it to death]" (Rom. 8:7, KJV). Such change involves our *will* momentarily, daily. *We* must consign our flesh to the cross. In Galatians 2:20 the word is, "[We] have *been* crucified"—something done to us. But in Galatians 5:24 it is, "[We] have crucified"—something we do to ourselves. Herein is balance, for it is both that we are crucified and that we crucify ourselves. We help Him do it to us. The minister must coach but never do so much that the person fails to put himself upon the cross.

Transformation is not complete until we treasure all our life and praise God from a full heart for it. The end result is that we are grateful for everything in our life, for we see that whatever happened was blessing in disguise, either sent or at least allowed by God. The Father knew what degradations we would choose to fall into, what would be put upon us and how we would respond, and in His predestinate will planned in Jesus Christ to transform dust and ashes to love and joy, ugliness to beauty, and weakness to strength.

The Spirit of the Lord God is upon me, because the Lord hath anointed me to preach good things unto the meek; he hath sent me to bind up the brokenhearted, to proclaim liberty to the captives, and the opening of the prison to them that are bound; to proclaim the acceptable year of the Lord, and the day of vengeance of our God; to comfort all that mourn; to appoint unto them that mourn in Zion, to give unto them beauty for ashes, the oil of joy for mourning, the garment of praise for the spirit of heaviness; that they might be called trees of righteousness, the planting of the Lord, that he might be glorified.

—Isaiah 61:1–3, KJV

CHAPTER 8

BITTER-ROOT JUDGMENT AND EXPECTANCY

See to it that no one comes short of the grace of God; that no root of bitterness springing up causes trouble, and by it many be defiled.

—HEBREWS 12:15

Do not judge lest you be judged. For in the way you judge, you will be judged; and by your standard of measure, it shall be measured to you.

—MATTHEW 7:1–2

Do not be deceived, God is not mocked; for whatever a man sows, this he will also reap.

—GALATIANS 6:7

BURT AND MARTHA CAME to me (John) for ministry. Burt thought the problem was pure and simple—Martha was too fat, and he couldn't stand it! Martha felt awful about herself but claimed it wouldn't be so hard to get the fat off if Burt would just quit criticizing her all the time. A few minutes of questioning revealed some root causes. Burt had grown up with a mother who not only became obese, but was also slovenly. She failed to care for her appearance. The house was poorly kept. And she would use the toilet with the door open and the children running in and out. Burt judged his mother for her appearance and habits. His bitter-root judgment and consequent expectancy was that his wife would become obese and slovenly.

Martha had grown up with a father whom she could never please, no matter how much she tried. He always found something to criticize; at least, that was her perception. Whether her father was actually that critical was not what was important to me as a prayer minister. What was crucial was that she had judged her father. Since she could not honor her father in that area, life would not go well for her in all similar aspects of life (Deut. 5:16). Her bitter-root judgment and expectancy was that the man of her life would always be critical of her; she would never be acceptable or be able to be pleasing to her man.

When Burt and Martha met, Martha was a slim and beautiful girl. They fell in love and married. Later Martha became pregnant. As she grew in size, so did Burt's difficulty to appreciate and compliment her. After delivery it took a while to lose the weight. Burt became increasingly upset and critical.

Burt now was sure he had married someone like his mother (though he couldn't have consciously admitted that inner realization). He found himself increasingly critical and scolding. But that was, of course, what Martha already expected would happen! Under attack, she became agitated and insecure, so she ate more for comfort—and grew heavier. As Burt became angrier and more critical, she became more upset, more nervous, hungrier, and fatter. All of this affected her ability to keep herself and the house neat. Their judgments and reactions spun to more and more painful levels, until at last she was living with an angry demon, and he was living with a blimp!

What created such a destructive spiral? It was not merely psychological expectancy. It is true that he expected his wife to become fat and she expected to be criticized. But psychological expectancy by itself lacks sufficient power to have overcome their determinations to lose weight and to stop criticizing. They had already seen what they were doing to each other before they came. Being Holy Spirit–filled Christians, they had set their wills to quit. They came because they found themselves powerless to stop. They knew they needed help.

The law of judgment does have that kind of power. When Burt judged his mother, the law that declares that the measure he metes out he must receive went into effect. When his judgment dishonored his mother (regardless of whether she merited his judgment, even if his judgment was true), that meant that Deuteronomy 5:16 ensured that life would not go well for him in that regard. Most cogently, his judgment was a seed sown that, by law, had someday to be reaped. Just as a tiny mustard seed grows to produce a large tree, so a seed of judgment sown increases the longer it remains unrecognized and unrepented of. So we sow a tiny judgment and reap again and again, larger and larger in life.

Every time we do a deed or hold a judgment in the heart, that can be compared to throwing a ball against a wall. If a physicist knows the weight and size of the ball, the distance to the wall, and my hurling power, he can predict when and with what momentum the ball will return. That is natural law. We comprehend that easily enough. But God has not made one law for the natural and another for the spiritual. All things are governed by the same basic laws. The law expressed in physics is, "For every action there must be an equal and opposite reaction." In chemistry it is expressed, "Every equation (or formula) must balance." In moral and spiritual life it is, "Whatsoever a man soweth, that shall he also reap" (Gal. 6:7, KJV), and "Judge not, that ye be not judged. For with what judgment ye judge, ye shall be judged: and with what measure ye mete, it shall be measured to you again" (Matt. 7:1–2, KJV). All things will come to resolution and balance (justice). It is one basic law, described differently in each field.

The law of sowing and reaping, however, adds another dimension. We do not sow one seed and get back one seed. All things increase in God's kingdom. God desires increase in all beneficial things. The first command given to Adam and Eve was to be fruitful and multiply and fill the earth (Gen. 1:28). The man who buried his talent was reprimanded by our usually gentle Lord Jesus for not at least putting his talent where it could increase: "Then you ought to have put my money in the bank, and on my arrival I would have received my money back with interest" (Matt. 25:27). The longer a judgment continues unrepented of and unconfessed, the greater increment it gains. We sow a spark and reap a forest fire, or sow to the wind and reap a whirlwind. When the Word says, "The measure you give will be the measure you get," I think perhaps it means "in the same regard or area of our life," rather than the same amount (otherwise the Word would contradict itself).

The loving-kindness of God our Father is that He moves on us again and again to prompt us to do some good thing. When we finally act, He lets us reap a hundredfold as though it were all our own idea. He sends servants on Earth and in heaven to persuade us not to do some bad thing, but when we do it, He moves heaven and earth to cause us to repent and confess so He can reap all our evil for us in His Son, Jesus, on the cross!

The law of sowing and reaping was eternally in operation for the entire universe before Adam and Eve were created. Before the entrance of sin, the law was designed to bring multiplication of blessings—and it still does so today. But the advent of sin meant that the same law from then on rebounds to destruction. Therefore, the Father, knowing from the ground plan of Creation what men would do, planned to send Jesus to reap the evil we deserve. In diagram 1 below, we can see how our judgments return upon us. Proverbs 13:21 says, "Adversity *pursues* sinners, but the righteous will be *rewarded* with prosperity" (emphasis added). The law of God actively causes reward and punishment to come upon us, as surely as any other natural law exacts its due.

Diagram 1

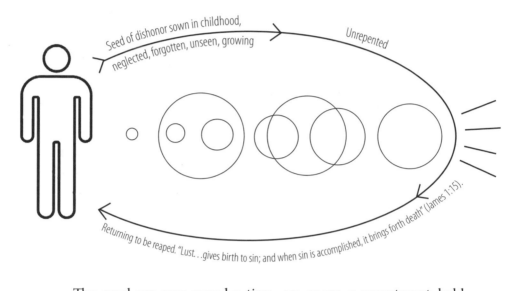

The seed we sow may be tiny—an anger, a resentment held against some family member as a child—and forgotten. The longer it remains undetected or neglected, the larger it grows. So we may sow a Ping-Pong ball and reap a nine-story bowling ball!

The grace of Christ on the cross delivers us, as diagram 2, on the following page, shows. Colossians 2:13–14 says, "Having forgiven us all our transgressions, having canceled out the certificate of debt consisting of decrees against us and which was hostile to us; and He has taken it out of the way, having nailed it to the cross." There is no cheap grace. Every sin demands resolution.

Diagram 2

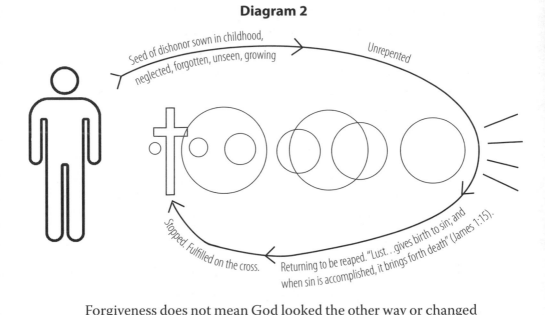

Seed of dishonor sown in childhood, neglected, forgotten, unseen, growing

Unrepented

Stopped. Fulfilled on the cross.

Returning to be reaped. "Lust…gives birth to sin; and when sin is accomplished, it brings forth death" (James 1:15).

Forgiveness does not mean God looked the other way or changed His laws. Jesus said, "Do not think that I came to abolish the Law or the Prophets; I did not come to abolish, but to fulfill" (Matt. 5:17). The full legal demand of the law of sowing and reaping was fulfilled in pain upon the body of Jesus in anguish in the heart and soul and spirit of our Lord upon the cross! (See diagram 2.)

Nevertheless, the cross is not automatic. If we do not repent and confess, we reap in full despite the fullness of mercy available at a moment's utterance.

Since Burt had judged his mother for obesity, he was due to reap obesity—who would be a more likely person through whom to reap than his wife? His judgment played upon her already latent tendency toward a weight problem, tempting her to gain weight. His necessity to reap what he had sown was therefore returning to him like a mighty wind. For Martha, that was like standing against a hundred-mile-an-hour gale, tempting her to gain weight. In this way, Hebrews 12:15 is often fulfilled: "And by it [a root of bitterness] many be defiled."

But Martha had her own set of judgments, which first drew her to marry a man who was likely to criticize and then pushed him to do so. Her seed sown ripened and was reaped through Burt.

Burt and Martha, like most couples, found that they were designed to grind against one another's problems. His judgments exactly matched what she was most likely to become, and her judgments matched his carnal tendencies.

Burt and Martha are not unique. We have found bitter-root judgments and expectancies in every couple to whom we minister! Bitter-root judgments are the most common, most basic sins in all marital relationships—perhaps in all of life. These three simple laws affect all life:

1. Life will go well for us in every area in which we could in fact honor our parents, and life will not go well in every area in which we could not honor them.

2. We will receive harm in the same areas of life in which we have meted out judgment against others.

3. We will most surely reap what we have sown.

We regard these laws as the most powerful keys that God has revealed to His people for the healing of relationships. These three laws are the basis of almost all our prayer ministry.

Most couples enter into a relationship with little or no awareness of what they are bringing with them in the heart or what power those unconscious forces have to influence, drive, and control perceptions, attitudes, and behavior.

A Model of the Problem

At the beginning of my marriage with John, I (Paula) had some awareness that I was imperfect, unfulfilled, and needing completion.

But like most young brides I felt I was beginning my new life rather clear, clean, and fresh. I had no idea what a large and complex bundle I was bringing into that new life. Like multitudes of Christians, I did not understand that though my sins had been forgiven, I was still the shape of the person my experiences in life and my reactions to them had made me to be. I did not know I would be inclined to "see" my husband and relate to him according to the attitudes and expectations of my flesh until, in Christ, I could experience interior cutting free from the past and growing into the new life. The weighty contents of that bundle, which included my nationality, culture, race, creed, religion, parents' training, modeling of parents, sibling rivalries, hurts, wounds, fears, joys, judgments, skills, successes, failures, hopes, dreams, shoulds, and should nots, dragged me down to prevent uninhibited sharing of myself. They were also at times the trigger points for ammunition to be hurled John's way.

Another factor had to be dealt with. I held an ideal image of who John was and had to be in order to complement me. I tried hard to be the person I thought I was and liked to think I had succeeded in some measure. It was my hope that John's shape of person would fit mine comfortably. Where I had weaknesses and undeveloped areas, I earnestly hoped he would be strong and capable so as to fill and strengthen me. Where I had areas of natural skill and strength, I hoped he would have the decency to stand back and give me room to express myself. I thought our coming together should be as effortless and painless as possible.

We had not been married long before I discovered that we were not at all shaped for a struggle-less coming together as one. It was obvious that the closer we moved to one another, the more we were going to have to make adjustments. It took awhile for the two of us to realize that we were both a mess and that it was part of God's plan in calling us together that we should grind blessedly against each other's character and so become polished and perfected.

God gives us a beloved enemy to force us spiritually lazy people to face what is undealt with in our flesh, else we would go through life ever congratulating ourselves that we are OK without Him.

Unfortunately, what happens in many marriages is that when couples begin to grow close enough to one another that the grinding and polishing process is going on in earnest, they withdraw from the pain, erect defensive walls to hide their vulnerability, and find themselves in a marriage filled with symptoms of defense and flight. The husband lives on his side of the wall, spending more and more time at the office, immersed in hobbies, playing golf—anything to avoid prolonged exposure at home where it hurts—and he looks for places to express himself where there is no threat to his ego. The wife pours herself into her children, spends her time at crafts, clubs, and church, and talks to her women friends about the things she no longer feels it is safe to confide in her husband. Being together becomes excruciating, as it seems only to accentuate the loneliness they both feel in isolation from one another. Occasionally they may throw rocks at one another from behind the wall: "If you would only change, I'd be all right!"

The world's culture feeds them continually with lies. "If it feels good, it is right." "Love is warm and fuzzy and makes you feel tingly all over." "If you were really in love, you'd be living happily ever after." "If you aren't happy in a relationship, get out of it." Their marriage certainly doesn't feel good, and they begin to think, *We must have made a mistake. I have the wrong partner. God never intended for us to be together.*

And so one or the other (or both) wanders from the marriage in search of that "ideal partner," that "soul mate," who must be out there somewhere. The wandering partner may indeed find someone who initially makes him "feel good." But because he has not let the Lord deal yet with the things in his heart, he will choose that new relationship with the same eyes, the same sensitivities, and the same criteria that equipped him for choosing in the first place. And should he marry a second time, the moment the new mate begins to penetrate his heart, he will find himself repeating the same patterns all over again. More cogently, the same necessity to reap seeds of judgment not yet stopped on the cross will most likely still draw a mate through whom to reap, usually more detrimentally. In this way some people go from marriage to marriage to marriage—right on to dead-ended frustration: "I guess I'm just not marriage material." (By the same token people go from church to church and from group to group and from friend to friend, searching endlessly for someone to make them feel good with no challenge to grow and change.)

There is only one answer for any marriage or any vital relationship. That is to exchange that dividing wall of hostility for the cross of Christ. It is to stop all demands that the other person change. It is to die daily to self, to continually ask the Lord, "What in me is contributing to the breakdown of this marriage?" "Lord, why doesn't my mate get better just by living with me? What is there in me that needs to die? Bring me to death." It is to confess, "Lord, I can't be loving to John, but You can. Give me the love You have that I may give it to him." "I can't forgive, but You can. Express Your forgiveness through me." It is to ask the Lord to enable compassionate identification with the other's hurts and fears, and wisdom to minister to those feelings. Identify and deal with past issues on the cross of Christ so that they no longer have any power to affect what lies ahead. Embrace each step of God's sometimes painful plan to transform your life as you live with your mate and work through problems together.

If one partner in a marriage refuses to enter into that process of transformation in the Lord, all is not lost. The unbelieving partner is sanctified through the believing partner (1 Cor. 7:14). What happens in the heart of one affects the other, if not consciously, at least beneath the level of consciousness. Eventually it will bear fruit. The more immediate effect of one partner's finding a stopping place on the cross is just that; the vicious cycle is stopped. The remaining partner may continue to behave in the same old habit patterns, but those ways find no place to land in the Christian. They can no longer hook into sensitive trigger points.

I (John) was raised with a mother who was hypercritical. I judged her for that. My bitter-root judgment was that the woman of my life would always criticize and seldom affirm me. My mother also made me work long hours and then gave little comfort or appreciation for it, and so my bitter-root judgment was that any woman close to me would expect me to work long hours and then be unhappy with me anyway and insensitive to my needs.

I (Paula) was raised with a father who was a traveling salesman, gone two weeks at a time. Though my mind said, "I'm proud of my daddy; he is working for us," my heart sang a bitter tune: "Oh, yeah, why isn't he ever here for me when I need him?" I was covertly angry with men. My bitter-root judgment was that the man would always be gone from me. What better place to reap that than to marry a workaholic pastor!

It takes little imagination to see how we were designed to grind on each other. I (John) would work long hours for the church (whose symbol is mother or woman) and find myself constantly criticized both by the church and Paula. Paula would be angrier and angrier the harder and longer I worked to please. The power of law is such that had I not possessed a built-in workaholic structure, Paula's seed sown would have tempted me to become a workaholic, or in one way or another to be away from her. Her anger made me ask myself, "Who wants to come home to a buzz saw anyway?" My necessity to reap bitter judgment guaranteed that Paula would be tempted to criticize, had she not already been so disposed.

Not only was John a workaholic, but also he was always late. In the first years of our marriage, John came home from calling on parishioners habitually late to dinner. I would get after him, and he would promise to watch the time and try to arrive home promptly. But neither my scoldings nor his determinations helped. He seemed to have some kind of block about time. Time was just something not to be noticed. We ruefully laughed about "Indian time," while I hurt and hurt and grew angrier.

Then we learned about bitter-root judgment and expectancy patterns. I repented (solely by faith) of angers I had never yet (nor ever have) felt against my father, but supposed must be there, and asked the Lord to haul to the cross my bitter-root expectancy that my man would always be late. Then I could begin to remember a little red-haired girl sitting disconsolately, waiting for her daddy to come home on the weekend, being more and more disappointed as the seemingly endless hours dragged by. This was more difficult to see because my father, in actuality, was always punctual. But a little girl's grasp of time is not that factual. I repented and asked for a new heart. John soon found himself easily coming home on time—no sweat, no struggle.

My (John's) bitter-root expectancy from my judgment of my mother was that I would be criticized even when doing my best. And since no one can perform well under a critical eye, I had often as a child blundered absentmindedly or stupidly and had been criticized roundly for it. So both by judgment necessitating reaping and by psychological expectancy, I looked for the woman of my life to criticize me and expected to blunder into it continually. That trait was nicely matched by the fact that Paula was raised with three younger brothers. The first two especially were normal, rambunctious boys who were always into something that embarrassed their righteous older sister. They loved to tease her unmercifully—like running in to throw earthworms in her bathwater! Being adventurous, they got into a plethora of "dumb" scrapes. And who was it who did the dumb things that caused the teacher to make the entire class stay after school? Boys, of course. Who stuck her long red braids in the inkwell? Who threw paper wads and splattered ink? Boys! Paula's bitter-root judgment was that boys (men) would always do dumb things and get everybody into trouble. How better to reap that than through an immature, head-in-the-clouds, mystic, dreaming, absentminded preacher?

During the first years of our marriage, I suffered "hoof-in-mouth" disease. I was always saying some dumb thing. I preached on Sunday morning. Paula preached every Sunday afternoon! "Do you know what you said to those people?" It was so bad that each Sunday morning Paula would say, "You aren't going to say something startling today, are you?" and then of course I had to, just to declare independence. I even found myself continually inverting words, much to my consternation and embarrassment, like instead of saying, "Look up 1 Peter 3," it would come out, "Look up 1 Threeter Pee."

Then I was called to teach out of town, away from Paula. Much to my surprise, out rolled uninterrupted wisdom with no dumb-dumbs. I thought, *Hallelujah! I'm healed. Wait till I get back home!* Only to fall right back to spoonerisms and all kinds of blunders. Finally the Lord revealed that Paula's bitter root was defiling me, "and by it many become defiled" (Heb. 12:15). She repented of her judgments on her brothers and other men and boys and asked that the Lord give her a new heart, crucifying the expectancy that men would do dumb things. Since then I have never suffered more than the normal goofs anybody makes, and they are my own, not her reaping.

My (Paula's) bitter-root judgment and expectancy that the man would leave me matched John's workaholic nature in another way. John would always be finding someone to help, sacrificing too much family time for others. Though that was actually out of order (God was calling him to first priorities, his wife and children), John had that one neatly masked under noble serving for God. God wasn't calling him away from home. As a boy he had had to be out milking cows, feeding chickens, and doing chores while the rest of the family played and visited, and he had formed a bitter expectancy that life would always go like that. That perfectly matched my judgment of men. It was so bad that even on vacation, five minutes after setting up our own camp, John would be out walking through the camp-ground finding someone else to help—and I was furious!

REAPING WHAT YOU SOW

Law is so powerful that, unless the cross intervenes, the requirement to reap what was sown can overcome our strongest good natural capacities. My (John's) mother was part Osage Indian, part English. Both cultures have produced very reserved people, and it was not easy for her to express emotion or affection. I judged my mother for not giving enough affection. So the expectancy was that I would be a suffering-servant martyr who would work long hours, only to be criticized and then not receive enough expressions of love. But I married a butterball of affection! In seminary I had determined to be a secluded scholar, but Paula would come and sit on my books on my lap and express affection to me. I protested while lapping it up! In five years that didn't happen anymore. Paula was no longer that affectionate. Why? My bitter-root judgment had to be reaped. Law made it exceedingly difficult for her to maintain her good inten-tions. My necessity to reap (plus psychological expectancy) sorely tempted her to stop giving affection.

My (Paula's) father was seldom home to protect me. Those three rambunctious brothers gave me a hard time (no tougher than normal—actually quite healthy teasing, as brothers will do). But my heart was bitter. No man would be there to defend me. I would have to do it all myself. John grew up with stern, English training to lay down his life to protect a woman. He had seen his father live that in many ways for his mother emotionally. And there is scarcely a stronger or fiercer trait in Indian nature than for a brave to defend his wife! By both inheritance and training, one of his strongest char-acteristics was to defend a woman, especially his wife, against all attacks. He found himself totally bemused that something almost always blocked him so that he seldom was able to defend me. I had sown seeds, and the reaping was so powerful that it overcame his strongest good intentions.

Women who are raised with alcoholic fathers and judge them for it often either marry a man who is already an alcoholic (they are used to that, and it confirms their judgment), or their man sooner or later becomes one. And so it goes—weak father, weak husband; poor providing parent, poor providing husband; cold and distant father, so is the mate, and so forth. If the husband does not fit the pattern, either the little girl did not judge and so is not forced to reap, or, having judged, has been delivered from reaping by the grace of God.

Men whose mothers were domineering attract the same kind of woman, unless grace intervenes. Men whose mothers often left them with babysitters, or alone, due to sickness, marital separations, or death find wives who do the same to them. And so it goes— cold, insensitive mother; cold, insensitive wife. If the condition is not exactly the same, the parallel is unmistakable. Again, not the actual history is important but whether the child judged the parent. Reaping is then inevitable. Either Jesus is allowed to pay the full legal demand and so set us free, or we reap, usually through the mate.

When one receives Jesus Christ as Lord and Savior, all that bitter-root system is dealt a deathblow. But observe that St. Paul was writing to *Christians* when he *commanded*, "*See to it* that...no root of bitterness springing up" (Heb. 12:15, emphasis added). Note the words "springing up," like a plant suddenly appearing from a hidden root. He did not say, "Lop off visible branches," or "Deal with the obvious," but rather see to it that no (hidden, beneath the surface, problematic) root become manifest and cause trouble.

Sometimes, repentance prior to accepting Jesus as Lord and Savior has reached to a bitter root, so that the moment of conversion is also the moment of deliverance. Most often, however, vast subterranean taproots and spreading, hidden tributary shoots remain untouched until we obey St. Paul's command to get at them.

We wish we could train every minister or lay leader, on principle, to look for bitter roots in each person in every ministry session. Physicians are trained to examine meticulously for certain possible conditions routinely, especially in first interviews. So also do dentists, chiropractors, and other professionals. Paula and I routinely ask questions concerning early childhood, checking to see whether bitter roots lie behind conditions.

"You say your husband never listens to you? Tell me about your father. What was he like?" After a few basic general questions, such as, "Did he give you affection? Was he 'home' when he was home? Did he stay with your mother? How did they relate to each other?" we will ask, "Could you talk with your father? Could he hear and understand you?"

In nearly every instance in which a husband will not listen, we find the same began with her father. "Oh, he was always too busy. He never listened to me."

"Your wife is always sicker than she really is, and it grates on you, and you can't make yourself help her like you should? What was your mother like? How was your mother's health?" It is amazing how often the response is, "Oh, she was always complaining about this or that ailment and taking to her bed," sometimes accompanied by, "She made Dad wait on her hand and foot," or "I hated that."

His statements may be, "My wife can't keep the house neat," or "The laundry's never done," or "She's always shopping and spending too much money," or "She gossips too much. Always talking."

Then our questions will be, "How did your mother take care of the house?" "Did your mother keep your clothes clean and ready when you were a little boy?" and so on. Usually we ask several other general questions first and then slip in the relevant ones so as to camouflage our intent so we are sure the person is giving us honest answers.

The woman may make these responses: "He won't ever take me out anywhere; he just sits in his darn ol' easy chair and falls asleep," or, "He never notices whether I look nice," or "He never disciplines the children; he just abdicates and leaves it all up to me."

Then we will ask her, "Did your father do things with the family? How about picnics or fishing trips…things like that?" "Did your father like to do things around the house, or did he get lost watching TV or sleeping a lot?" "Who wore the pants in your family?" "Did your father or your mother do the disciplining?"

Sometimes it was not the father who failed a daughter and was judged, but the mother, but the grown wife is reaping through her husband. Or sometimes we reap through the children, or another person who lives in the home or nearby, or a boss, pastor, or colleague at work. Sometimes, likewise, a son may have judged his father but reaps through his wife.

Sometimes patterns of judging and reaping are not so obvious or so neat and clean. For instance, a little girl may have felt greatly rejected by her father. Questioning reveals, however, that her father seldom was gone from the home, had no great obvious vices (such as alcohol, violence, or a critical tongue), attended church regularly, was a good moral man, and so forth. But perhaps he was inattentive, or one who fled into books or seldom spoke. A girl may just as easily take those simple flaws as rejection but finds it difficult to fault her father since "love" and "loyalty" cover feelings of hurt. All of what she can remember is rosy. She may marry a man who insists on remaining in a teenage gang mentality, frequently leaving her in order to go out with the guys. Or he may be alcoholic or a workaholic. Whatever the surface manifestations, it is the same root—one way or another he fails to take note of her, and she feels rejected.

As much as we wish we could train every prayer minister to look for bitter roots, we would hope to induce each to look for crossover patterns. We could almost make it a hard and fast rule: whenever one partner has a bitter root, the other will have something exactly matching! A prayer minister or lay leader ought to suspect that possibility simply by the law of attraction and repulsion. We manage to attract to us and are ourselves attracted to those whose characteristics closely match or oppose ours. After watching this phenomenon through forty years of ministering to hundreds of people every year, Paula and I are still amazed at the consistency of law and of human nature.

Sometimes it is not through others we reap but through Mother Nature, circumstances, or our own selves. For instance, I (John) have seen cases in which several generations suffered business failures, sometimes by ineptitude but often by accidents, economic depressions, weather, or other factors. Generational sin (Deut. 5:9) may not fully explain the strength of such a pattern, whereas bitter-root judgments by sons upon fathers may turn out to be the main way a particular generational pattern continues to descend.

BITTER-ROOT JUDGMENT

In cases in which a person is reaping upon himself, another law usually is foundational: that we become like the one we judge. Romans 2:1 states, "Therefore you are without excuse, every man of you who passes judgment, for in that you judge another, you condemn yourself; for you who judge practice the same things." In our hearts we all practice the same sins. Although we have not all committed adultery, what person has never lusted in his heart? Jesus equated this with adultery (Matt. 5:28). Although we have not all committed murder, what person has never hated anyone? John equated this with murder (1 John 3:15). Therefore, we must not judge another. Judging is akin to unforgiveness, and Jesus said that if we do not forgive, we will not be forgiven (Matt. 6:15). Therefore, as long as we judge another for a particular sin, the same sin remains in our hearts, unforgiven. The law of increase will then cause it to grow: "For they sow the wind, and they reap the whirlwind" (Hosea 8:7). Thus, when we judge another, we doom ourselves increasingly to commit the same sin as the one we judge (or something so similar the root cannot be missed). For example, a wife who exclaims, "My mother was always shouting at us kids. I swore I would never act like that. And now I'm doing it just like she did, only worse!"

This insight has become one of the most common and helpful keys we use when ministering to people's hearts. So often we become what we judge, or we do what rankled us in the behavior of others, that to us it has become a "law" based on God's law of Romans 2:1 and the other scriptures we just cited. As routinely as doctors check blood pressure, we check to see what roots of becoming like what we have judged may be lying behind unwanted fruits.

Sue found herself horrified that though she swore up and down she would never harangue her husband as she saw her mother do to her father, now she couldn't stop her tongue—and her normally gracious husband had "had it." He had retreated to his woodworking hobby, manifesting Proverbs 21:9: "It is better to live in a corner of a roof, than in a house shared with a contentious woman." Afraid she would lose him altogether, she came seeking answers. When she forgave her mother and received forgiveness for judging her, we could pray together to haul her practiced habit of critical speaking to death on the cross. She became affirming and delightful to live with, and her husband came in to be with her—which is what he had always wanted anyway.

Rob wanted to be the kind of boss employees would like to joke with and hang out around. But his workers never seemed to be around him more than they had to. He had been trying to control what he would say: "But no one can tame the tongue; it is a restless evil and full of deadly poison" (James 3:8). Management courses had offered a number of behavior modifications, and he had tried to do them, but nothing worked. Frustrated and lonely, he came to us. It took only a few minutes of questioning to see that he had detested the way his father could "never" affirm him and "always" had some "helpful suggestion" that turned out to be critical and wounding. We have learned to watch out for those words—*never* and *always*. They are often sure clues to a heart that does not see both sides of reality, a heart that is bound up in judgment. Rob had become what his father had been. His mind was determined to affirm his employees, but it is out of the heart that issues rise, so the practices of his heart continually submerged his good intentions. The answer was simple. When he forgave his father and was forgiven for judging him, we could bring his practiced habits of criticalness to death on the cross and impart to him loving and positive ways of relating. Needless to say, he became a friend at work, and people loved to be around him.

It is not merely that we become what we judge. Bitter roots, by the law of sowing and reaping, act like boomerangs to bring on us exactly what we judge others for, or something so similar we can't help seeing it when a prayer minister discovers it for us. Our son Mark had been conducting his own practice of prayer ministry in Florida. Now he knew it was time to come home and be a part of Elijah House. He and Maureen had been scraping by financially, and their old rattletrap car was hardly worth bringing to Idaho— even if it could make it that far. So I told him to sell it. I looked around until I found a "cream puff" (an older car in perfect condition). I bought it for him and presented it as a gift, so proud and pleased with myself. But it was winter, and Mark had become used to driving in Florida. That beautiful car lasted four days! Mark slid on the ice into an oncoming car and totaled the cream puff. Thank God neither of them was hurt. But I was thoroughly upset. I knew better than to judge Mark, and tried not to, but couldn't help doing so anyway. A week later I slid our new Honda Accord on the ice into the rear fender of a Jeep and did $3,700 worth of damage to my car, to say nothing about the Jeep. No one had to tell me how to add two and two and come up with four. My judging was a sowing, and the reaping was almost immediate.

I ministered to a young man whose father had been an alcoholic and was unfaithful to his mother. The young man had hated those things in his father and swore that he would be different. He loved his wife dearly. He had become a Holy Spirit–filled Christian, attended church regularly, read his Bible, and loved Jesus. Now, seemingly inexplicably, he found himself compulsively going out to drink, and he had already committed adultery. Guilty, worried, and confused, he came to us. A few minutes of questioning revealed the bitter-root pattern of judgment. Though Christian, he had never distinctly repented of his judgments against his father. That doomed him by the power of law to do exactly as his father had done. Jesus, of course, longed to protect him from himself, and after he fell, Jesus longed to set him free. But free will prevented our gracious Lord until the young man could see his roots and repent specifically. Under our advice and ministry, he did so repent and was set free.

Of all the keys the Lord has given us for understanding human behavior, this legal requirement to reap what we judge in others is perhaps the most common and incisive. In fact, we say, "If you want to know what's troubling a preacher, listen to what he preaches about!" We don't mean that critically, and the "preacher" may not be a pastor, but a mother who rants at her children or a father who blows up and can't be as patient with his children as he has always wanted to be. Or a friend who can't be a friend, whose mouth continually undoes his loving intentions. Or the "preacher" may be a teacher whose classes become filled with rancor, whom nobody likes and who will become the joking remembrance of alumni reunions in the years to come. *What people rave about in the behavior of others is often the sharpest clue to their own judgments and struggles.* Look always at the childhood. Whom did the person judge so that his or her behavior manifests the same today?

BITTER ROOTS FROM THE WOMB

Sometimes bitter roots lie hidden far beneath levels of what we have commonly thought of as "rememberable" incidents. One lady came whose behavior totally baffled her. She loved the Lord and her husband. She believed the Bible, belonged to a solid evangelical church, and was Spirit-filled. Now she found herself compulsively leaving her husband to go out drinking. She had become involved in a fully adulterous affair with an alcoholic married man whom she did not even like or want to be near! Her husband was a gentle, loving, born-anew, Spirit-filled man. "Whatever in the world am I doing?" she cried out. "And why?"

So I asked first about the parents who had raised her (unaware that she had been adopted). Her adoptive parents were wonderful parents. They had given her affection and good discipline and were themselves without harmful vices. I could not track her present behavior to any discernable roots severe enough to cause such inexplicable behavior. It didn't make sense, so I asked more questions. Eventually, it came out that she had been adopted. She had thought that since she had no conscious memories of her biological parents, it was irrelevant that she had been adopted and had not even mentioned it.

Her biological mother had never been married, and at forty had dated an alcoholic married man! He had not told her that he was married. When she became pregnant and informed him, he vanished from her life by returning to his wife and refusing to acknowledge any connection with her. Her mother carried her for nine months, in bitter anger against the father and in days when condemnation of out-of-wedlock pregnancies carried more shame. Before giving birth, her biological mother decided to give her up for adoption. The young girl had never known her biological parents. Later on, her adoptive parents informed her of her adoption, not wanting her to be shocked by finding out on her own and then hurt later.

That was what made her present behavior so confusing to her. She thought, as most do, that what children experience in the womb is unknown to them and has little affect. Nothing could be further from the truth.

In our spirits we know and react to what is happening around us while we are in the womb, just as John the Baptist, six months along in Elizabeth's womb, knew Mary had entered Elizabeth's home and was pregnant with our Lord. John leaped for joy in his mother's womb. So this incident in Luke 1:41–44 makes it clear that, as infants in the womb, we do know things and react.

In this lady's spirit in the womb she had reacted to her mother's fornication, her father's alcoholism and adultery, and his rejection of her mother and her.

Before we continue, perhaps we should address some of the common questions asked about prenatal issues. (A more complete discussion can be found in our book *God's Power to Change.*) Many churches believe in the "age of accountability," usually understood to be about the age of thirteen, when Jewish children come of age at their "bar/bat mitzvah." Consequently, there are those who believe that a child before that age is not capable of sinning. But that is not what is meant by the "age of accountability." It simply means that a child is not yet held accountable. If he sins before that age, God will deal with his parents. After that age, God will deal with him directly.

Scripture is clear that children do sin. Proverbs 20:11 says, "It is by his deeds that a lad distinguishes himself if his conduct is pure and right" (inferring that the opposite also can be true; that his sins make clear he is not pure and right). Proverbs 22:15 says, "Folly is bound up in the heart of a child, but the rod of discipline will drive it far from him" (NIV).

But how early can a child sin? Some would say, "Not very," based upon the false notion that all sin is conscious and intentional. But the Church has always recognized that there are sins that are neither conscious nor intentional. When we speak of prenatal "sin," we are not saying that a child in the womb has consciously and intentionally sinned by judging another. Rather, when children react and judge in the womb, it is sin, but not to be blamed as though consciously intended: "But if [a] person sins unintentionally..." (Num. 15:27, NIV) says, and goes on to say that such sinning is not to be judged as we would for intentional sins.

But can a child in the womb sin unintentionally? Scripture says, "Surely I was...sinful from the time my mother conceived me" (Ps. 51:5, NIV). Psalm 58:3 says, "The wicked are estranged from the womb; those who speak lies go astray from birth." Like John the Baptist, we are aware of much that happens around us while we are in the womb, and like him we can react. John the Baptist reacted with joy, but we can react in many sinful ways, such as with resentment and judgment.

In this lady's situation, her judgments (whenever they were formed) led her to sinful reactions, which doomed her to:

- Reject someone (her husband) just as she was rejected
- Drink
- Commit adultery

Why "doomed"? Because the laws of God are irrevocable and unstoppable in power. In more than forty years of practicing prayer ministry, we have found it to be one of God's immutable laws that when a person judges another, that judgment dooms him to do either the exact same thing or a similar sin from the same root. That is why this woman, who didn't even like the taste of alcohol or the man she was dating, did so compulsively.

Another woman, whose prenatal history was nearly identical, also came for prayer ministry. Her mother had also committed adultery and carried her in shame in a strict, religiously condemning society. Her father had also rejected both the mother and her. Now, though she had married the man she loved and had conceived in holy love and joyous expectancy, she found herself amazed and dismayed that instead of welcoming and loving the child in her womb, she hated her unborn baby. She couldn't understand why. She had expected to relish being pregnant and to be able to love her baby fervently—and here she was despising it! Why? Questioning soon revealed her prenatal history. She had felt her mother's shame and rejection and had hated herself in the womb. Unaccountably, children at most any age manage to blame themselves when their parents quarrel and reject each other—"Oh, if it hadn't been because of me, they wouldn't fight." They think in the heart (below the level of conscious thought): *It's my fault they're fighting*. So this woman hated herself in her mother's womb. Happily, almost always, when pregnant women have been enabled to understand this and have forgiven their parents and themselves, true godly love for the baby in their womb returns, full force, and the women are better for the experience and the freedom of heart that has resulted.

HELPING THOSE WHO FAIL TO SEE

The most pathetic thing Paula and I see daily in prayer ministry is that day by day, year after year, good Christian people are driven by forces of which they have no awareness! We are not speaking merely of libidinal psychological forces. Those are bad enough that most any psychiatrist or psychologist could agree with that statement. All kinds of counselors have discovered the truth of Ecclesiastes 1:18: "Because in much wisdom there is much grief, and increasing knowledge results in increasing pain." Beyond such grief is a depth of pathos for ministers, for we see not merely psychologically but by the invincible operation of inevitable laws of judgment, especially of sowing and reaping, acting with impersonal, unrelenting force in human life (short of the cross of Christ). The pathos is because Christians ought to believe, should know and see, and let Jesus Christ do what He came to do—to set them free.

But Christians have failed to see. If this book has no greater purpose than this chapter, it is enough if Christians will only come to see how the law of sowing and reaping affects them drastically, day in and day out, in multitudinous details in common daily living. It is absolutely necessary that each believer learn to think in terms of the operation of God's law in his or her daily life. You must see and understand how what you did as a little child (or are doing as an adult) can be like a boomerang, swishing to return with ever greater momentum in the present or future. Unless you are able to comprehend that every action in life must reap a result, you will find yourself continually being hit on the blind side and smashed by events, and wondering why. Life will seem unfair. It is to help you, and the entire body of Christ, to see in order to repent and stop the reaping of destruction that we write this chapter. Oh, that men will hear!

No law of God is an inert, dead thing. The laws of God will operate whether we know of them or are ignorant, approve of them or disapprove, love them or hate them, believe or disbelieve. God's impartial laws will affect us whether we unintentionally activate them by judgments as children or intentionally sin as mature people. It makes no difference. Law is law. If we disbelieve, what we think or feel about the reality and effectiveness of the laws of God will have about as much effect as a gnat trying to knock down the Empire State Building! The laws of God will roll right on, controlling the universe no matter what our puny minds think or don't think.

The law of sowing and reaping is so simple it is deceptive. We just don't think anything that simple can be that real, that pervasively powerful and effective. Perhaps for that reason St. Paul warns, "*Do not be deceived*, God is not mocked; for whatever a man sows, this he *will also reap*" (Gal. 6:7, emphasis added). It is impossible to hold a judgment or do a deed without setting in motion forces that absolutely must return to us. If a man were silly enough to believe with great certainty that he could fly, the law of gravity would not be affected one whit! He would plummet as surely as the foolishness of his technique allows. Only the operation of devices within other laws enables a man to fly. Just so, a thief will eventually reap, no matter how brilliantly he escapes human detection. A secret adultery will result in destruction of the soul and in later reapings, no matter what modern *"feelosophies"* say. The law of sowing and reaping guarantees unconditionally that no one ever gets away with anything at any time in any place!

If you do come to see that the law of sowing and reaping is so effective, you will be prepared to use it as a key for understanding human life and dilemmas—within your own life and in the lives of others. But remember to include the dimension of time in your reckoning, for reaping is not immediate. As a farmer must wait first for seeds to die and rise, then to grow, then to bloom, then to form in the head, only at last to mature, so reaping in all of life must wait.

There is one crucial difference between the farmer and the minister. A farmer not only can see his plants growing and that some tending may be required, but for the minister, in the case of bitter-root judgments sown in childhood, most commonly seeds sown are forgotten. Seldom can the shape of bitter-root judgments be seen in earliest childhood. Thus, if our sinful sowings have never been fully consciously admitted, it seems inexplicable to us when reaping arrives as a whirlwind when the sowing to the wind was so long ago, so small, and so hidden or forgotten. People condemn one another and themselves for failure. To struggling, suffering people, it seems unfair that sins of judgment sown in infancy can destroy adult relationships. But that is because we attach blame to a process in which there is none, only impartial law.

When man was created and set in the garden to take care of it, law already had long regulated growth. In that innocent order, all things did indeed work together for good (Rom. 8:28, now only by the cross, then without need of it). The good deeds of Adam and Eve rebounded to increase the blessedness of Eden, and there were no sinful seeds setting in motion terrible later reapings. The entire universe was designed for "the building up of itself in love" as does His Church (Eph. 4:16).

But since law is impersonal, when Adam and Eve opened the door to sin, every succeeding generation has reaped the result! That means that infants come into a fractured and sinful world with hearts already corrupted by Adamic sin, and so make judgments and hateful reactions that must later be reaped in vast increase—by the same law that would have brought ever-increasing blessing, had Adam and Eve never sinned! God does not blame. He knew before anything was ever created that men would fall and that the very laws He had built to govern all things in blessedness would be turned to bring destruction. So from the ground plan of Creation He predestined Jesus to reap all harm, to pay on the cross all the price demanded by His own impartial law.

Is Life Fair?

We must understand, especially as prayer ministers and lay leaders, one vitally important fact: human free will is so precious to our Lord that He will not let the efficacy of the cross be applied to us without our consent. It is as though He has brought us a present on Good Friday but wrapped it up until our own invitation allows our own Easter morning to open it to personal application. In each detail of our life it is the same. Our gentle Lord is always standing outside some new sequential inner door, softly knocking, but the only latch is on our side. Bitter roots are normally not taken care of until we invite Jesus to accomplish that specific task. Our compassionate Lord hurts more, not less, in the waiting until we do. He pays the price even for our tardiness in confessing.

Is it fair that a tiny child should live with an angry, violent father and reap thereby a life with similar bosses or with a husband who acts out the same, only worse? Of course it isn't. Whoever said, since the Fall, that life was fair? On the other hand, should infants reap, all undeserved, all the benefits of their fathers' fathers—house and health, technology and medicine, appliances, clothing, rich foods, knowledge, and spiritual blessings, and then be exempted from reaping the harms that come in the same package? God is just and fair. Life on Earth since the fall of Adam and Eve is not.

So it is that tiniest children, who hardly can be blamed for making angry, bitter judgments at parents who may richly deserve such evaluations, nevertheless set in motion forces that must move to resolution. It is not that God is mean and picks on children. It is the opposite, that God in His kindness and compassion sees the gathering storms from all our sowings (though we may see neither the sowings nor the impending reapings), and He moves, unseen by us, to intercede on our behalf. When the prayers of others on Earth and the intercession of heaven fail to gain access to our stubborn flesh, then despite the perfect will of God, we reap what we have sown.

Jesus always lives to intercede on our behalf (Heb. 7:25). "For I, the LORD, do not change; therefore you, O sons of Jacob, are not consumed" (Mal. 3:6). Let all Christendom understand that were the Lord to change—that is, to stop interceding for one short while—the weight of our sowings of sin is so great that "this tape [earth] will self-destruct in five seconds!"

Destruction is reaped not merely in our marriages and in our families, but in all aspects of life. As a child, a friend of mine had a father who had continually gambled away the family money. When our friend went to work around the age of eleven or so for the family, if his father could find the money he earned, he would steal it and gamble it away. He judged his father for that. His bitter-root judgment was that his father (therefore, subsequently, all businessmen) would cheat, lie, and steal. Needing partners for his real estate projects, he continually drew to him men who failed him one way or another—lying, cheating, being lazy, and leaving our friend to hold the bag, unaided. In his business office he managed to find partners who invariably failed him. One split his family in two. Being determined, he searched and found a man of faith, a most highly recommended man, a born-anew, church-attending, responsible deacon. This man so failed to be responsible in business that our friend was almost driven to bankruptcy. While our friend was in the hospital with back trouble, this partner went to his doctor, lawyer, and prayer minister (me) to try to have him declared incompetent so that he could steal the business!

Subsequently, we talked of his judgments against his father and how his bitter root was being reaped through all these men. He repented and was forgiven. In prayer we called that bitter root to death on the cross and prayed for a new heart, a new expectancy by which to draw to himself dependable, honest men. One by one the Lord has weeded the leeches out of his company and brought to him men of honor and dependability. Recently his banker, extending a sizable loan that saved his business, said to him, "Now that you have gotten rid of those men and are running your company again [he meant out of the hospital and back on the job], and now that you have around you these men we can trust, we will back you again." Our friend's bitter root nearly destroyed his business, but the cross of Christ saved it.

Note the words, "and by it many be defiled" (Heb. 12:15). Our bitter root, by the force of reaping, actually defiles others. We defile them to act around us in ways they might successfully resist apart from us. Every married person or other kind of partner ought to ask, "How come the other didn't become a better and stronger person by associating with me?" And, "Can it be that my bitter root is defiling?" "Am I reaping something through this person?"

We need to understand, however, that guilt is always found on both sides. Our bitter root could not overcome the other's free will unless something in him is still flesh (no matter how good and strong) or weak and sinful. Although I am 100 percent responsible for tempting someone to react, the other person is 100 percent accountable for his reaction.

DEALING WITH THE BITTER ROOTS

When you become aware of a bitter root in your own life or in the life of someone to whom you have begun to minister, there are several factors that will need your attention.

First, there is the original event. The grown person to whom you are ministering may have no awareness, just as Paula has never been able to feel any kind of resentment against her father. But we are not dealing first with feelings of the flesh or spirit. We are dealing with facts and law, by faith. Forgiveness for the sin of judgments should be pronounced if present circumstances indicate reaping. Where reaping is, judgments and/or sinful actions were the sowing, no matter what the other's reasoning mind or feelings may protest. As you pray with the person, that person need not feel anything during ministry or prayer. You are acting as confessor, offering assurance of forgiveness and ministering beyond the adult to the wounded person within. Forgiveness needs to be said several ways so that the inner one can take hold and receive.

Ask the individual both to forgive and to accept forgiveness, purely by faith if necessary. Forgiveness is essential. Without it, no subsequent healing can happen (Matt. 5:23–24; 6:15; Mark 11:26).

Reactions to the original event(s) created structures in the character. These are practices of judgment and psychological bitter-root expectancy that only the cross can transform. Pray aloud with the person to whom you are ministering, asking that Jesus' work on the cross be applied to that practice in the flesh. It will help, and may be necessary for the individual to say in prayer, "I hate it. I reject it. I don't want it."

Years ago, a science-fiction movie told the story of a spaceship lost upon a planet devoid of its former population. A second spaceship, sent to find the first, found only a professor (the scientist aboard the flight) and his daughter still alive. Soon members of the second crew began to be torn apart one by one by an only partially visible monster. The captain discovered a machine invented by the former population. By placing a cap on the head and turning the machine on, great mental powers were released. Unfortunately, so were all the inner powers. The hidden demonic urges of the former population had thus materialized, causing them all to destroy one another by their covert hatreds!

Meanwhile, all members of the new ship's crew were being destroyed until only a few remained, locked behind a supposedly impenetrable door with the scientist and his daughter. Now the demonic thing was smashing through even that! At the last moment the captain, perceiving the truth, called on the scientist, whom he discovered had tried the machine, to realize it was his own despotic thing, jealously overprotecting his daughter. At last the scientist stepped in front of the door and cried out, "I hate you. I reject you. I don't want you." Dramatically the sounds of rending and tearing descended into silence.

I know of no better way to depict the power of such subconscious practices in our flesh, or how they can only be destroyed by holding them to the cross by hate. "Hate what is evil [loathe all ungodliness, turn in horror from wickedness], but hold fast to that which is good" (Rom. 12:9, AMP). Sometimes we have prayed with others about such practices, in full faith, only to have them continue, seemingly unabated. The missing factor that denied success was hatred of sin.

We spoke earlier of reward systems. All bitter-root systems contain rewards. I (Paula) grew up determined to serve well no matter whether my folks appreciated or criticized. Actually, that built a noble martyr who loved that stance. That fed my ego. No matter how much I protested that I disliked being criticized and was tired of serving for little reward, the inmost truth was that in reality I preferred it so. That proved me the magnanimous suffering-servant Christian, and all those others less than me, even hypocritical. So long as I enjoyed that reward, I was not about to let go and face as sin my defiling others by tempting them to act in an unchristian manner toward me.

So long as John kept working too late, spending too much time away from me and the children, my noble martyr self could "bear that cross" all alone and unappreciated while serving anyway. That fed my ego. So long as I enjoyed proving the man wrong, so long as I enjoyed being "one-up" (on my brothers in sibling rivalry projected onto John), so long as it was precious to me that my bitter-root view of life was being confirmed again and again, I had no real intention of letting go of my bitter root. The rewards were too sweet.

Perhaps now we are prepared to comprehend the necessity for the command, "See to it that no root of bitterness..." Sometimes overturning a bitter root requires upsetting the entire stance of life by which one has defined his life and found his (fleshly) worth. It may mean coming to hate that fleshly righteousness by which we have congratulated ourselves that we are the good guys standing for Jesus and being persecuted by all the dirty guys.

Further, real repentance may require that we repent of our pushing those very people whom we have been blaming for hurting us to do so by being in proximity to us. Oddly, we may have to repent that we hurt them by tempting them to hurt us! We may not become whole until we bless them for being the ones through whom we could reap! Truly, forgiveness is not fully fulfilled until we bless those who spitefully use us (Matt. 5:12–13; Rom. 12:14; 1 Pet. 3:8–9).

WATCH OUT FOR "GUERRILLA RESISTANCE"

Once you have experienced forgiveness and freedom from the bitter roots of the past or prayed with someone else and been a witness of the transformation in that person's life, be on your guard against the little tugs backward that can still occur. The big battle may be won, but there may be hundreds of pockets of "guerrilla resistance" here and there in your flesh. Habit structures are like morning glories, weeds that keep sending up sprouts from a long, persistent root system until every part of the old root is uprooted or finally too weak to send up a shoot.

The blessed end of transformation of bitter roots is first that we find ourselves continually surprised. Things just don't happen like they used to. New things happen. People compliment who didn't, or give affection, or whatever is the reverse of what used to happen. Good rather than bad "accidents" happen. Things begin to work together for good, visibly. One can't miss seeing it.

Perhaps the most blessed shock is that often the very people we have been hating become the ones we love or appreciate the most. We even become grateful for their former persecuting ways (or whatever they did) because by that we saw and were set free. Life takes on a new lease. It is as though new vistas open before us—and we come (slowly, perhaps) to realize they were there all along; we just couldn't see them. What used to bother us now falls like water off a duck's back. We giggle instead of tense up. We laugh with those we used to get mad at for laughing at us. And we see others and our own selves with real compassion.

Truly, in that area our hearts have come to experience what it is to be born anew.

CHAPTER 9

GENERATIONAL SIN

You shall not worship them or serve them; for I, the
LORD your God, am a jealous God, visiting the iniquity
of the fathers on the children, and on the third and the
fourth generations of those who hate Me, but showing
lovingkindness to thousands, to those who love Me and
keep My commandments.

—DEUTERONOMY 5:9–10

SOMETIMES EVEN THOUGH A believer has exhausted every
track of personal sin, perhaps even in a ministry setting for
a period of time, it seems that great trouble still besets that
person's life and family. It does not seem possible the tragedies that
continue could have had their origin in personal sin yet to be discovered. The answer is this: sometimes troubles originate from causes
outside a person's own guilt or flesh. Sin and its effects may descend
through family lines. We call that generational sin.

Generational sin and its effects come to us in three ways. We will take a look at each of these ways in this chapter.

GENERATIONAL REAPING THROUGH THE GENES

We inherit both good and bad through our genes. Far more descends through our physical inheritance than we may suspect. One Italian woman informed me that her doctor advised her never to allow her daughter to date another Italian because through her bloodline ran a tendency to a particularly tenacious variety of depression. African Americans have long suffered from sickle-cell anemia. Physicians routinely question diabetic patients concerning a history of diabetic or blood disorders in their families. Heart disease, back disorders, tendencies to lung conditions, allergies, and so forth are known to descend as physical weaknesses or tendencies.

Job 17:5 says, "If a man denounces his friends for reward, the eyes of his children will fail" (NIV). We need to be careful not to assume that *every* person who wears glasses had some ancestor who told lies against friends for false gain! But this scripture does give us a clear instance of descent of a particular physical condition as a direct result of the sin of an ancestor; ergo, *some* people who have eye trouble *may* have had ancestors who were dishonest. These things are clues for prayer ministers and lay leaders who seek to lay the ax to the root.

Not only do physical conditions descend, but also personality and behavioral tendencies do so as well. As a child, I (John) was such an absentminded dreamer that when my folks would send me upstairs to get something, not only did I often forget what I was to get, but I also forgot I had been sent to get it! Pretty soon they would have to send someone else after it—and me. By the time I was eighteen I had largely outgrown that. But our son Mark followed exactly in my pattern. He would fall into a daydream on the way to school, kicking cans and leaves along the walkway. At noon the school office would call to ask, "Where is Mark today? Is he sick?" Paula would find him somewhere halfway to school, totally oblivious to reality. In the morning one of us might walk by Mark's door and happen to observe him pulling on a sock. Half an hour later, there he would be—in exactly the same pose—catatonic, lost in a dream world! He had never seen my example. We had not discussed it. Where did it come from? Genes, of course.

About age twelve, I had a penchant for brushing my teeth. After every meal, or any snack between meals, I would rush to the bathroom to brush my teeth. The entire family would be sitting in the car, motor running, and someone would ask, "Where's Jackie [my nickname]?" And the exasperated reply invariably was, "In the bathroom brushing his teeth!" Long before my marriage at twenty-one, that habit was totally forgotten and never mentioned. Precisely at the age of twelve, Mark not only took up the exact same habit, but he also carried toothpaste and his toothbrush in his pocket in case he ate something somewhere!

Johnny caught Paula's stubbornness; Ami, my mystic nature. What family has not marveled at the way peculiar characteristics have traveled seemingly by no other possible route than through the genes?

Brothers and sisters separated at birth and raised in different families in altogether different cultures have discovered, when reunited, similar likes, dislikes, talents, weaknesses, mannerisms, and habits, which could have come from no other source than physical inheritance.

There is a mystery connected with the loins that far surpasses our understanding: "And, so to speak, through Abraham even Levi, who received tithes, paid tithes, for *he was still in the loins of his father* when Melchizedek met him" (Heb. 7:9–10, emphasis added). The mystery is only partially solved when we come to understand that the Hebrew worldview is quite different from our own. They had a corporate understanding of community and family. In their culture, it was understood that what one person does affects all, including his descendants, for better or for worse. Thus, all of Adam's descendants were negatively affected by his sin. Our own sins affect future generations. (See Deuteronomy 5:9.) On the other hand, blessings are also passed down. Jacob blessed his twelve sons (Gen. 49), and centuries later, the twelve tribes descended from them were still living out many of those blessings. But Paul's statement about Levi seems to extend this principle farther than our Western minds can stretch. In some unexplained way, Levi blessed another through his ancestor, although he was not present at the time.

Let me share from my family history. I (John) was raised in Missouri and Kansas, where there was a great deal of racial prejudice. Ethnic jokes were standard fare at most gatherings. I didn't see African Americans serving anywhere else but as housemaids and janitors! Being a normal kid, I wanted to be like everyone else, and, being as sinful as any other, I tried to hold the same prejudices. But I couldn't. For some unknown reason I found I loved African American people. To me they were unaccountably beautiful, and I liked to be around them. I still do. I couldn't understand why it hurt me so deeply when people told ethnic jokes.

While Paula and I were working our way through seminary in Chicago, I drove a taxi at night and went to school during the day. Just prior to my starting on this job, some white drivers had been held up in black neighborhoods, and one had lost his life. The air was full of fear. The law required that a cabbie take a fare wherever the passenger desired. Whenever a driver was requested to take a passenger into one of the black areas of town, he would lock his doors, roll up his windows, and deadhead (i.e., travel without a passenger) out of there, sometimes not even stopping for stop signs. That meant by the law of supply and demand that much business was available in those neighborhoods. Consequently, I drove there most of the time. Drivers all around me told stories of being harassed by African American customers. That was never my experience! We visited and chatted merrily. Other cabbies told of being "stiffed" constantly (that means not to be given a tip—cabbies depend on tips for their livelihood). The people in those neighborhoods tipped me as generously as anyone else.

Fellow drivers in my garage were held up. One particular driver was taken into the sticks (far out in the suburbs, away from any cab stand), whereupon a gun was placed against his neck, followed by a harsh, "Gimme your dough! Nice shirt, buddy. Hand it over. Nice pants…" My buddy wound up standing barefoot in his shorts in sub-zero weather at 2:00 a.m., watching the thief drive off with his cab!

In those days I was a foolhardy, adventurous nut who wanted to be held up just once, just for the experience of it! I couldn't even accomplish that! God protected me! The African American passengers I drove for were thoughtful, courteous, and protective of me. On one occasion, I drove an African American man who had a fresh bullet hole through his shoulder next to the clavicle; his accomplice could have stolen my cab and perhaps injured me, but all they wanted was a doctor, quick! On another night police pulled me over and hustled my burly passenger against the cab and frisked him, finding a big pistol! But he turned out to be a night watchman on his way to work.

I seemed to lead a charmed life. I never was hassled by anybody. I knew next to nothing about faith in those days, but enough to know that God was using these African American passengers to protect me. We had a grand time together. I couldn't understand what made me so different from all my buddies in the garage.

After being born anew and filled with the Holy Spirit, I was drawn particularly to minister to African Americans. One, Rev. Ev Carter-Spencer, became a spiritual daughter to Paula and me.

Then my father came to live with us. He had so hated his tenure as a marine in the First World War that he would never talk about his war experiences. But one night he opened up and began to share. As an eighteen-year-old, immature lad off the streets of Joplin, he had been placed as a guard over hardened criminals on their way to the front for their last chance to serve honorably. Upon arrival in France, his captain ordered the entire company to step forward as he called their names. Dad's name was the only one not called. Apparently his guard duty had set him apart and caused the roll call officers to forget him. He inquired of the captain, who responded, "I have no orders for you, son. Just wait here until orders come." Whereupon the captain marched the company away and left Dad standing alone and frightened on the docks in a foreign country at war!

Dad looked around and found two companies serving as stevedores. One was a white company made up of men who were mostly from the streets of New York. Many had been gang toughs and still tended to get into knife fights with little provocation. The other was an African American company, who chanted as they worked. The men of this all-black company took my dad in, fed him, gave him a place to sleep, and protected him until the roll officer remembered him and sent him off to the front.

As my father told the story, my spirit was leaping! I now knew why I had always felt gratitude in my heart for African Americans and why I had loved to listen to their songs! Somehow, like Levi, I was blessed by my ancestor's dealings with others. I expected to feel safe among African Americans during a time of racial unrest, although I was not there when they protected my father. How can this be? Such mysteries belong to God. But thank God, generational blessings belong to us. Surely more blessings descend than we are aware of.

I also was raised in a strongly Protestant region, in which much anti–Roman Catholic sentiment prevailed. Catholics were going to take over the world! Catholic churches had guns in their basements, and the pope would persecute Protestants wherever he could get the power! Never mind that historically my own denomination (Congregational) did not allow anyone not a member of the Congregational Church to vote in Massachusetts until after 1834, while Maryland, a Roman Catholic state, gave freedom of religion and power to vote to all! Prejudice says, "My mind is made up; don't confuse me with the facts." I am as sinful as anyone and wanted to share in anti–Roman Catholic stories. But again, I couldn't. I hated to hear stories of hate and prejudice. I found great respect for the Roman Catholic Church welling up in me, and I wondered, *Why?*

After the baptism of the Holy Spirit, I found myself ministering often among Roman Catholics and loving it. In my youth I had attended only one Mass, on a Christmas Eve. The sanctuary was so crowded that I had to stand in the narthex, peering down a long nave at a man mumbling something unintelligible in Latin. The man behind me was so drunk that I was high on the fumes! Wonder of wonders, whenever I subsequently attended a Catholic Mass, my spirit soared in worship and sang within itself, "I'm home. I'm home. I love it." That totally blew my mind. I could not understand why I felt so much sense of belonging. I still love a Catholic charismatic Mass far above all other forms of worship. Why? This Protestant never expected anything like that!

Then the elders of the church I was serving said, "John, you are getting too tired. Don't go on any more teaching-healing missions unless you take a team along to protect and support you." I was to go to Tiffin, Ohio, to a Christian camp, but I couldn't find anyone free to go. At last, only our daughter Ami and one Catholic laywoman could go. This was to be that lady's first occasion to act in a ministering capacity in a Protestant gathering, for she would help me with the prayer ministry. She was none other than Barbara Shlemon, who became one of the leaders of the Catholic charismatic movement and author of *Healing Prayer*.[1]

We arrived in Tiffin a half-day before camp was to start, and, having seen an interesting church as we drove in, we decided to walk across town to find it. Ami and Hal Spence Jr., son of the chairman of the camp, went with us. As we entered the sanctuary of St. Mary's Catholic Church an anointing came upon me the like of which I had never, or ever since, experienced! It was so full and powerful

I thought I might translate—and wondered if hitting the ceiling on the way up would hurt!

Ami took one look at me and said, "Dad, what's happening to you?"

I said, "I don't know."

We sat down to pray. The Lord then revealed that He had brought Barbara and me together, along with Ami and Hal for support, in order that we as a Catholic laywoman and a Protestant minister might pray for the healing of the ill effects of history and reconciliation of Roman Catholic and Protestant churches. We were to pray through the entire history, from 1515 to the present, in mutual repentance, asking for forgiveness and praying for healing for all the hatred, wars, prejudices, confusions, broken and divided households, suspicions, disrespects, and so forth. All week, we spent hours in prayer together, proceeding through all the history we could remember, applying the blood and the cross of Christ.

On July 23 we prayed for the healing of every occasion in which Catholics and Protestants had married, only to be cast out of one or both churches. We prayed for families to be healed, divisions overcome, and unity restored. That day being my birthday, my mother called to wish me a happy birthday. I told her, "Mom, I'm doing part of what God commissioned me to do," and told her what Barbara, Ami, Hal, and I were doing and how we had prayed that day for intermarriages to be healed.

She said, "Oh, Jack, you never knew. I never told you. All the Osages of your family line were devout Roman Catholics. They attended Mass every morning. Your grandmother, my mother, was a strong Catholic during her youth. When she married Frank Potter, your grandfather, she was *churched* [a colloquialism that meant to be excommunicated or put out of the church]. That's why you have always known her as a Methodist. She became a Methodist shortly after they were married." By one of God's coincidences, I had prayed for the healing of my own beloved grandmother that birthday and on the same day discovered my own unsuspected heritage in the Catholic Church!

At last, I understood why I loved African American people and the Roman Catholic Church. I share these stories in hopes that many may find revelation, or at least mysteries to ponder, in thinking about their own heritages. Surely we should give thanks and praise for all the blessings that have come down to us through our family heritages.

Unfortunately, however, it is not solely blessing that has come down to us from our ancestors. As we shall see, we need to bring all of our past to the cross, even the blessings, that the good may be filtered and the detrimental stopped altogether.

GENERATIONAL SIN THROUGH EXAMPLE

The second way sin descends is by example. We have taught this in every book and tape we have produced, that children learn to become *what parents are* rather than *what they teach*. We do not need to expand on that again here, but it is a principle of great importance. But let the reader not think brevity signifies lesser importance. How could anyone not see that our formation with our parents perpetuates sin in our lives and in the lives of our children and grandchildren? Example writes what we become, unless grace intervenes, all the way back to Eden and forward to our Lord's return. It is the primary reason why fathers' hearts must be turned to children and children's to fathers, lest the earth be smitten with a curse.

GENERATIONAL SIN THROUGH SOWING AND REAPING

The third way sin and its effects descend is perhaps the most cogent, if not in the long run the most influential—the law of sowing and reaping. Reaping for sin is seldom immediate. It is also never without increase: "For they sow the wind, and reap the whirlwind" (Hosea 8:7). Time, though not the only factor, remains a major reason why children reap what fathers, grandparents, and great-grandparents have sown.

When David sinned, his child died (2 Sam. 12:1–24). When Josiah humbled himself before the Lord, the prophetess Huldah told him, "You shall be gathered to your grave in peace, neither shall your eyes see all the evil which I will bring on this place" (2 Kings 22:20)—which meant, of course, that he would not reap, but his children would! A rather dubious blessing!

It may seem unfair that unborn children, years later, are required to suffer the effects of the law for sins committed by ancestors who may even be unknown to them. Of course it is not fair. God is fair, but since sin entered God's world, life is not fair. God has worked from the beginning to reestablish His justice through the cross of Christ. He suffers far more for our injustices than we who cry out the age-old cry, "It's not fair!"

God established the law of sowing and reaping before sin entered the world. The law was designed to increase blessing. As men labored and sowed to the Spirit (Gal. 6:8), they were to reap blessing. Thus the universe, like the Church, would build itself up in love (Eph. 4:16). But when sin entered, those same impartial laws of sowing and reaping and of increase worked as dispassionately and inexorably to bring destruction. Now, when men sow to the flesh, they reap corruption (Gal. 6:8) from the very laws that were designed to bring them blessing!

So it is that, despite God's first will, which is always love and blessing, the good will of God, which is impartial law, also binds God to abide by its actions (since He obeys His own laws). Wherever men will let Jesus Christ reap the dire effects of law through forgiveness and atonement on the cross, God can prevent tragedy. But, as I said, even He has set Himself to obey His own laws. So whenever men will not repent, and by that fail to give Him access, men must reap, generation to generation, whatever is sown, however unfair that may be to the unborn and however much our loving God doesn't want that to happen.

Furthermore, every material blessing we enjoy has come down to us from the labors of our ancestors. We reap every blessing fully unmerited. Did any of us invent the cotton gin or the looms that have spun our comfortable clothing? Did we produce central heating or air conditioning? Did we discover the medical advances that have saved our lives and wiped many diseases from the face of the earth? Who among us invented his own combustion engine or fashioned his own automobile? How about dishwashers, washing machines and dryers, toasters, and microwave ovens, to say nothing of gas and electric ranges? Apart from material things, how much have we reaped without effort from education, the glory of music, the beauty of art, and the fun of wholesome comedies, novels, and theater in general? Every good thing we enjoy has come to us as unearned increment—even the printing press, the paper, the easy chair, the light, and the ability to read, which enable us all to gain whatever knowledge this book offers at this moment!

Shall we say, then, that it is fair of God that we should reap every good blessing we have in life from the labors of our ancestors, but unfair if we also reap from their sins? Is it somehow God's fault, or is life to blame, when human sin abrogates the will of God and generations to come suffer its sad effects? Sin is to blame. And sin before that. And before that. All the way back to poor Adam—and Satan at last! In this we see the contest of the ages, wherein God would make amends for the sin of one of His creation! He Himself suffers our death due to our sin and brings to naught the work of Satan in bringing death. In Jesus, the Man of Nazareth, the God of life restores blessing where sin has reaped death.

God is more than fair; He is unfathomable love and healing to a world that deserves nothing but destruction and death. Immature children cry out that life must be made fair. Those who are wise praise God from a full and willing heart of thanksgiving, in the midst of an unjust and crooked world.

It is when we discover that destruction often rains upon people when nothing inside them any longer attracts it that we recognize that generational sin may be the cause.

THE EFFECTS OF GENERATIONAL SIN

We first discovered generational sin when a lady came to us in depression and fear. She was one of thirteen children: nine boys, four girls. Not finding full explanation of the source of her problems in her own life, I felt led by the Holy Spirit to ask about her entire family. Every one of her brothers had become an alcoholic, and some had died early in tragic circumstances. The last brother was a Satanist. Each of the women was mentally ill, except the woman to whom I was ministering, and she herself was dangerously close to it.

We saw patterns of rejection and divorce throughout the family. All the men in the family were either being destroyed or were already dead. Whenever such a pattern emerges, indicating destruction upon the males of a family, we call that an *ahaseuritic*. In the story of Tobit, in the Apocrypha, any man who married Sarah, daughter of Raguel, wife of King Ahaseurus, would be torn apart that night by the demon Asmodeus (Tobit 3:7). (Since we use this as an example, not the scriptural base of the teaching, we feel free to refer to the Apocrypha, which is regarded by Protestant scholars as inspired but not equal to canonical Scripture.)

I prayed with the lady about her family. About two years later, a bishop of an Episcopal church asked us to speak to a charismatic gathering in his diocese. We taught about generational sin, testifying in disguised form about that lady's family and how we had prayed for her. After the talk, a woman approached us and said, "You don't recognize me, do you?"

I said, "No."

She said, "I'm the one whose story you just told!" I couldn't believe it. That woman had been skinny and haggard, ashen, with stringy hair. Here was a beautiful woman, ruddy of complexion, well built, healthy, and vital! She went on to report that after our prayer she had gone through a time of trial in which she had to walk in a discipline of affirming God's presence and power in her life. Since then she had been watching her brothers and sisters leave alcohol and come to the Lord one by one. She exclaimed, "It's been like watching popcorn!"

Since that first eye-opener, Paula and I have regularly checked the family background of people to whom we minister. We may say, "Did your father have brothers and sisters? How many? Start with the eldest and tell me the salient facts—health, marriage, children, longevity, tragedies, divorces, and so forth. Now the next uncle or aunt, and the next." Finally, "How about your grandparents?" That done and duly noted, we ask the same questions concerning the maternal side. And then concerning their own brothers and sisters. We look for recurrent patterns, both of blessing and of harm.

Sometimes divorce runs rampant. One man came who was the result of his mother's third of five marriages. His mother was one of twelve children. His father was one of twelve. Among all those relatives, not one had been married only once. Most of them had been married several times! He was himself failing in his third marriage. Sometimes there are patterns of diseases, miscarriages, or early deaths. Sometimes there are closed wombs or only male or only female children born in a family. Abraham opened the wombs of Abimelech's people, for the sin of Abimelech had closed all their wombs (Gen. 20:18). Sometimes drugs or alcohol beleaguer generation after generation. One man came whose great-grandfather had tragically died at age thirty-nine, whose grandfather had tragically died at the same age, whose father had died in the same way at the same age. He was then thirty-eight, and counting down.

In my (John's) family, on my father's side, my grandfather had been a wealthy lumberman and bank president. During the Depression, he tried to carry his friends and lost everything. My father was indicted for a crime a man in his employ had committed, and though he was acquitted, court costs and fees cost him all he had and bankrupted his business. My brother Hal entered a business that folded and plunged him into debt. Coincidence? Not likely. We prayed for that pattern to end on the cross, and subsequent business ventures succeeded.

On my mother's side, the Osage Indian tribe was moved in 1869 and 1870 from eastern Kansas to northern Oklahoma. The white soldiers who were conducting them, knowing how fiercely Osage braves defend their wives and daughters, raped some of the women, seeking to provoke the men to battle as a pretext to destroy the tribe. The Osages could do nothing but seethe in bitterness. Thus took root a bitter judgment that worthless white men would take advantage of Osage women.

The tribe was governed at the time by councils of wise and prayerful men. The tribe settled in Osage County and made it law that any Osage allottee could sell his 770 acres, but whatever existed in the air above or the ground below would belong to the entire tribe, no matter who privately owned the land. When oil was discovered in Osage County, the entire tribe became wealthy all at once! Worthless white men then wooed and married young Osage women in order to live in luxury from their oil payments. Many were alcoholic, beat their wives, and were selfish and lazy. It is suspected that some killed their wives in order to inherit their allotment. Thus the bitter-root judgment and expectancy became ingrained that men who married into an Osage family would be alcoholic, lazy, unable or unwilling to support their wives, violent, and generally worthless men.

I do not know whether, or to what extent, any other families among the Osage were affected, but in our family that pattern was an unmitigated curse. My father was a good man but succumbed to the pattern. By the time I was ten he had become an alcoholic and was unable to support the family. My aunt married a man who became a medical specialist. His $30,000-a-year income would have been equivalent to more than $100,000 to $150,000 today. But he refused to support the family and was alcoholic and violent. My aunt finally divorced him. Her daughter married the same kind of man her father was and divorced him. My parents had one daughter. She married a man who was gentle but hopelessly alcoholic. He failed to support her. She went to work and supported the family. He sat at home and drank himself to death. They had three daughters. Each of my nieces married the same kind of man and divorced him. My brother, Frank, had three daughters, two of whom followed the same pattern. The only one who did not was adopted from another line. Our daughter Ami's first marriage ended in divorce. Not one woman in our bloodline escaped the pattern.

Now these effects of generational sin have been shattered on the cross, and succeeding generations are being set free. My aunt's daughter married well. My sister did not remarry, but her daughters have all remarried well, and so have my brother Frank's two daughters. Our daughter Ami remarried a wonderful Christian man. Our younger daughter Andrea, who had not married before we prayed, has since married a wonderful Christian man.

OCCULTIC GENERATIONAL SINS

Occultic sins create the most destructive patterns we have seen. In checking family histories in order to stop generational sin, Paula and I routinely ask whether anyone in the family has been involved in the occult. For occultic sins, the law requires, "I will also set My face against that person and will cut him off from among his people" (Lev. 20:6). Immediately the law begins to operate, so that the blessing of God is withdrawn, and succeeding generations reap multitudinous ways of being cut off. In some, the male line, which, of course, carries the name, ceases—no male children are born, or tragic deaths or divorces prevent succession. In some, financial tragedy occurs in generation after generation. The telling mark of descent of harm from occultic sin is that there is a curse upon the family. Whatever shape it takes, whether deaths, divorces, finances, illnesses, accidents, or other tragedy, it is not difficult to see a pattern—a design behind these happenings. Happenstance plagues all of us occasionally, but in these families so much happens so interconnectedly that even impartial observers are forced to admit, "This is too much—it can't all be coincidence!" Truly there is a curse that is irrevocably prescribed by law! "I will cut that man off."

Descent of that kind of harm by sin is not at all affected by whether we believe in God or His laws. Laws of the universe operate whether we know about them or not, believe or don't believe in them, want them or reject them. We will not affect the law; it will affect us! Abimelech was neither a Hebrew nor a believer in the God of Abraham. But he had sense enough to know there are laws that affect us, and he cried out when Isaac had said that Rebekah was his sister, "What is this you have done to us? One of the people might easily have lain with your wife, and *you would have brought guilt upon us*" (Gen. 26:10, emphasis added).

Abimelech knew firsthand what ravages come when law is transgressed, for Isaac's father, Abraham, had done the same thing to him, and Abimelech had taken Sarah into his household, intending to have sex with her, unaware she was Abraham's wife. God had come to him in the night then and said, "Behold, *you are a dead man because of the woman whom you have taken,* for she is married" (Gen. 20:3, emphasis added). Abimelech protested that he did not know. But then mark how even this heathen king knew how sin affects all under a man's charge. He exclaimed, "Lord, wilt Thou *slay a nation*, even though blameless?" (v. 4, emphasis added).

God replied that He knew Abimelech was innocent, and therefore He had kept him from touching Sarah, and that he should have Abraham pray for him, and he would live and not die (vv. 6–7). Abimelech did so: "And Abraham prayed to God; and God healed Abimelech and his wife and his maids, so that they bore children. *For the LORD had closed fast all the wombs of the household of Abimelech because of Sarah,* Abraham's wife" (vv. 17–18, emphasis added). Judgment had descended immediately! Law is absolute, upon Jew or non-Jew, believer or nonbeliever.

WHAT IS MEANT BY GENERATIONAL SIN?

You may ask, "Why didn't all harm stop when we died and were born anew in Christ? Why didn't our conversion end it?" Didn't the cross cancel our sins? Certainly it did! But personal sin is not the foremost reason why we suffer the effects of generational sin. Moses said, "Fathers shall not be put to death for their children, nor children for their fathers; each is to die for his *own* sin" (Deut. 24:16, NIV, emphasis added). Clearly, Moses believed that no one is personally guilty for their ancestors' sins. But Moses is also the one who introduced the very concept of generational sin and its consequences. Did he contradict himself? Not at all! For the concept never meant that we are personally guilty for our ancestors' sins. Rather, it meant that we are corporately guilty. At conversion, the cross cancels our personal sins, but it does not cancel corporateness!

So if the cross does not cancel corporateness, how are we to deal with generational sin? Not by conversion, but through prayers of repentance on behalf of our family lines. Perhaps, by God's grace, many generational sins are miraculously canceled without specific prayer, for the reaping we suffer appears to be far less than we deserve.

Nevertheless, we have ministered to hundreds upon hundreds of Christians who have been many years in the Lord who still suffered great harm from patterns of generational sin. These patterns were stopped and reversed to blessings when we discerned their source in their ancestry and brought an end to them through specific application of the blood and the cross of Christ.

We appropriate that sacrifice once and for all at the moment of conversion. But we continue to work out our salvation (Phil. 2:12). Sanctification is both completed and ongoing: "Because by one sacrifice he has made perfect forever those who are being made holy" (Heb. 10:14, NIV). Since dealing with personal sin is ongoing, and personal sin gives cause to generational curses, it stands to reason that such curses are also dealt with in an ongoing way, one repentance at a time.

Though we are positionally totally dead in Christ when we first receive Him, He has left it so that step by step we must reckon our flesh as dead on His cross (Rom. 6:4). In like manner, apparently we must see and stop generational patterns of sin by direct action in prayer. I personally cannot understand this, unless God knows we shall only be built up to stand as warriors in Him if we have to exercise discipline to claim our freedom. Perhaps it would be too much a matter of cheap grace, or too sudden a change, if everything were done all at once. Suffice it to say that the evidence for us is undeniable; we have seen countless longtime Christians suffer from generational patterns until someone by God's grace prayed effectively to stop that destruction.

Prayer for Release From Generational Sin

In sharing our way of praying about generational sin, we do not mean to offer a magic ritual or incantation. We encourage you to use our insights and our ways as a springboard to finding your own effective way to pray. Here are the steps we follow.

First, we spend considerable time asking people to relate as much as they can recall of the family history. As our questioning prompts their responses, often their eyes widen and they exclaim, "I never saw that. I never put two and two together until now. Look at that.

Every one of my uncles suffered tragedies, and so have my brothers. What did you call that?"

"An ahaseuritic demon—that's when all or most of the men are afflicted one way or another."

"Well, let's pray, before it gets me, too!"

In prayer, we place the cross between the person and his mother and father, their mothers and fathers, and theirs. We do that simply by stating it by authority in Jesus.

Usually, we begin the prayer by thanking and praising God for all that has come to us through our forefathers. We thank God for all the good we inherit daily. But then we pray that even the good be filtered through the cross.

We call for the blood of Jesus to flow back through the family bloodlines throughout their history, by forgiveness washing away the ground of Satan's attack. We ask in repentance for forgiveness for all sins, wherever possible (some things must wait for conscious repentance and confession).

Whatever patterns we have seen and discussed, we ask Jesus to destroy and transform on His cross. "The Son of God appeared for this purpose, that He might destroy the works of the devil" (1 John 3:8). We believe this to be the most important part of the prayer. *It is through unforgiven sin and consequent descending patterns that Satan perpetuates his destructions on families.* Wherever sin has allowed access, Satan enters to prey upon physical weaknesses, to exploit sinful tendencies, to cause proclivities to become addictions, proneness toward accidents to become tragedies, bad examples to become traps, necessities to reap to escalate to whirlwinds of destruction. "The thief comes only to steal, and kill, and destroy" (John 10:10). Family patterns are the handles by which Satan pumps the bellows of the fires of hell in any family. The greatest necessity in praying for the cessation of ruination in families is to stop generational patterns on the cross, calling for their death and transformation to blessing.

We name each pattern, describing it, and calling specifically for our Lord to destroy it. In this prayer, we are not merely praying for the person, but for him in proxy for his entire family. The person is the beachhead of heaven's attack upon the powers of darkness, and the land to be occupied is the person's entire family. We pray that whatever pattern we describe may be destroyed from the life of every brother and sister, uncle and aunt and cousin, grandparent and great-grandparent, and each adopted or in-law person connected to the family.

Many people have little or no knowledge of their family history. Adopted people especially may have no awareness. In such cases, we pray generally, and if the Holy Spirit gives a word of knowledge, we pray about that. A word of caution: some pray arrogantly about what they think they see, forgetting that St. Paul said, "We know in part, and we prophesy in part" (1 Cor. 13:9). The Revised Standard Version reads, "For our knowledge is imperfect, and our prophecy is imperfect." We do not always hear accurately. It does not hurt to say, "Lord, I think I hear You saying this, and therefore I pray that that pattern be stopped. If I don't hear rightly, Lord, I trust You to apply the prayer to what does need to be dealt with, or to reveal it later on more accurately so that we can pray again and so have the complete victory You intend." Humility is not lack of power, but gain.

Having prayed for destructive patterns to be destroyed, we are sometimes led to rebuke the powers of darkness and to command them to leave. Often I am caused by the Holy Spirit to bring forth this command in a loud voice. Sometimes, for reasons known only to Himself, the Holy Spirit, who is the general on the field, knows that *loud* authority is what is required: "In the days of His flesh, He offered up both prayers and supplications with loud crying and tears to the One" (Heb. 5:7). On many occasions, having prayed so for large groups, we have received testimony that at that shouted word of command hearers have felt powers of darkness leap away from them. People have testified then to feeling "breakthroughs," lightness and joy, freedom and certainty.

We ask Father God to send His angels to encamp about every member of the family (Ps. 34:7), to protect each one (Ps. 91:11–12), and to bring each one out of darkness into light (1 Pet. 2:9). We call for the Lord to send forth His warrior angels to do battle for the family.

Some time ago a heresy was taught that men should command the angels specifically, telling them what to do. Only God orders His angels. But we can pray to the Lord, asking Him to send His angels to minister to our families, to save them from harm, and to bring them messages of salvation. And we can believe that with or without the help of His angels, if we have faith, God will save us and all our household (Acts 16:31).

We believe that this key of overcoming generational sin is one of the most important the Lord has revealed to us and to other servants like us. Families languish in fear and harm who ought to walk free and easy in God's kingdom. We *can* set families free. Paula and I have received countless testimonies from people who have seen all the members of their families delivered and set free one by one after such prayers.

Prayers for the cessation of generational sin, like prayers for conversion, are normally one-time prayers. However, as bits and pieces of history are newly revealed, specific prayers about those revelations are not redundant. They are a continual working out and development after the first general prayer.

Whoever voices this prayer must know his authority in Christ as a child of the King. Powers of darkness do not yield territory to half-hearted mumblers.

God wants us to advance, occupy, and hold territory for Him. This prayer to stop generational sin is not merely for healing. Nor is it only defensive, as though stopping the encroachments of darkness were enough. It is aggressive warfare on the march to recover lost souls from the grip of darkness. It is a delight to all who enter the lists and challenge the champions of darkness.

> Let the godly ones exult in glory;
> Let them sing for joy on their beds.
> Let the high praises of God be in their mouth,
> And a two-edged sword in their hand,
> To execute vengeance on the nations,
> And punishment on the peoples;
> To bind their kings with chains,
> And their nobles with fetters of iron;
> To execute on them the judgment written;
> This is an honor for all His godly ones.
> Praise the LORD!
>
> —PSALM 149:5–9, EMPHASIS ADDED

CHAPTER 10

HEALING THE EFFECTS OF CULT ACTIVITY

Then I said, "Woe is me, for I am ruined!
Because I am a man of unclean lips,
And I live among a people of unclean lips;
For my eyes have seen the King, the LORD of hosts.
—ISAIAH 6:5, EMPHASIS ADDED

For by what he saw and heard that righteous man, while living among them, felt his righteous soul tormented day after day with their lawless deeds.
—2 PETER 2:8

See to it that no one takes you captive through philosophy and empty deception, according to the tradition of men, according to the elementary principles of the world, rather than according to Christ.
—COLOSSIANS 2:8

S EVERAL YEARS AGO PAULA and I were invited to teach in San Francisco. The other couple on the podium were cult deprogrammers who had made it their life's work to deliver men and women, young people especially, from the grasp of cults. They informed us that at that time they had been able to identify more than one hundred cults operating in the Bay Area alone! What has given rise to such a drastic increase in cult activity? Or have we only become aware of what has been happening all along?

It is hunger for authority, according to these deprogrammers, that serves as the lure for young people. In short, it is the absence of fathers. Multitudes of young people have slumbering spirits, which means that their spirits cannot discern the true from the false. At the same time, many also have great gaping wounds that cry for love, strength, and security from a father figure. Deprogrammers inform us that it is hunger for a father figure to tell them what to do that locks young people into being controlled by authoritarian cult leaders. Young people, despite their protests for independence, look for the security of being told what to do.

It is fear that rules and fear that chains. Fear of rejection. Fear of not belonging. Fear of punishment. Fear of "missing the Lord." Fear of "missing the kingdom." Fear of not living up to the Lord's demands (actually the warped regimen of the cult leader). Fear of reprisal if caught. Fear of being trapped again in the prison world of the parents and society. (Cult leaders portray everyone else as the prison and their way as the only freedom.) Fear of hell, pictured as waiting just outside the circle of the group. Cult leaders teach an expectation of persecution and say that the remonstrations of parents, pastors, and friends are nothing but persecution, confirming the leader's "righteous" stance. There is a fear not to be "in," not to suffer the outrages that confirm everyone else in the group as true suffering servants standing against this crooked and perverse generation.

Breaking Mental Strongholds

All such groups participate in and feed upon a paranoid messianic complex that identifies them as the good guys, the elect, the elite remnant who alone have the truth and must suffer for it.

It is not, however, merely psychological forces that captivate cult members. It is the power of corporate mental strongholds. It is thought control by powerful devices in our flesh. Mental strongholds are practiced ways of thinking we all share. They are not inert, like books on a shelf, ineffective until opened and read, but active monsters of energy that can clamp about the mind of a person until he can think no thought outside the parameter of the stronghold. Strongholds serve like cowboys, to run down any straying thought and turn it back into the herd. Their specific purpose is to prevent free thinking, to "take captive through philosophy and empty deception." It is the hold of strongholds, aided in their heinous task by the fears listed above, that must be broken by deprogrammers.

Our purpose here, however, is not to write a manual for deprogrammers. That is a separate field altogether, in which Paula and I confess little expertise. It is rather to teach the form of healing that should follow after the work of deprogrammers, lest the former cult member remain vulnerable to those who would lure him into repeated delusion.

Those who have been delivered from cults rightly fear being caught again. But that fear can turn into hypercaution, which may in turn prevent whatever wholesome associations would serve to provide needed nurture.

In the early days of Elijah House, one of our members had been a cult member. His fear of domination and control so monopolized his thoughts that he continually caused trouble in the group by falsely imputing to me and other leaders in authority motives and actions to control and imprison.

We failed to learn soon enough the lessons we now share. This man, still hungering for the very authority he feared, eventually left us and became caught up again in a rigid authoritarian cult.

A couple came out of a cult that insisted on intense shepherding and discipling. The leaders of this cult went so far as to insist on choosing who would be their friends and who would not. This couple entered Cornerstone Christian Fellowship, where our son Loren was the pastor. Many small groups were the very life stream of Cornerstone. This couple desperately needed fellowship and support but feared to enter any small group, unable by the numbing power of unhealed memory to discern that Cornerstone's small groups bore no resemblance whatsoever to the cult group that formerly controlled them.

It required patient teaching by Loren, loving fellowship, and soaking, healing prayer to overcome the deposits of cult membership. Former cult members remind us of crayfish, backing away with eyes bugging out and claws extended in defense. It may take many experiences of love and acceptance, despite cult members' tendencies to alternately attack and flee away, to reestablish the kind of trust that is the basis of all free friendship and fellowship. The key to the healing of former cult participants is long-suffering love. Former cult members are acutely sensitive to anything that remotely appears to manipulate and control them, while unconsciously, by bitter-root expectancy and judgment, setting up friends and acquaintances to do just that to them.

When long-suffering, forbearing love has laid the groundwork for receiving ministry, many simple acts of healing can follow. First, bitter-root judgment and the anticipation of being dominated and controlled should be brought to the cross, not only from the recent cult experience but also from early childhood parental frictions. Most importantly, such people need fathers and mothers in Christ. It was the very hunger for such relationships that trapped them under a despot. But since they now fear and flee from the very thing they most need, wise prayer ministers can simply fulfill the function without putting a name on it. Holding in the heart, loving unconditionally, being available, interceding continually, giving counsel without ever impinging upon free will, supplying as much affection as the other will receive—all these and more can be done without ever labeling such acts as father and mother tasks.

Deep, basic trust needs to be restored. These people must come to realize that it is again safe to unfold and bloom and that no one will curb, crush, or rip the tender petals. They must learn that it is OK to be vulnerable again, but not safe. We are never safe. Life always contains risk. They need to regain enough confidence and freedom in God to risk, to know He will restore us if we fail and do, in fact, get hurt again.

Ex-members of cults are uptight. They must have enough penetrative healing to their spirits so that they can relax from deep within and open to the winds and crosscurrents of life again. That is perhaps the most basic and needful healing of all, to restore the ability of the personal spirit to unfold, expand, meet others, and interrelate without excessive fear and guard-all walls. It is accomplished by praying aloud with the person for the Lord to comfort, to heal, and to restore trust as a sovereign gift, an act of His grace, a miracle of resurrection in the heart.

Their healing does require a miracle of resurrection. Like the man lame from birth whose muscles had so withered and atrophied that they had to be re-created and regenerated with power to run and leap (Acts 3:1–10), so the spirit's abilities have been so trampled and withered that one must call for a miracle of re-creation and rejuvenation. Like the man with the withered hand (Luke 6:6–11), former cult members have faculties that no longer can operate. Their inner being no longer can reach out and take hold, unless the power of the Lord's command enables the spirit to stretch out and venture again. Akin to the paralyzed man who was let down in front of Jesus (Mark 2:1–12), they possess many talents of the spirit paralyzed by fear. "And Jesus seeing *their faith* said to the paralytic, 'My son, your sins are forgiven'" (v. 5, emphasis added). Those who pray must have faith *for* such people. Their ability to trust has been paralyzed. God will answer the faith of those who pray, only secondarily the weak faith of the recipient.

HELP THEM REDISCOVER THE JOY OF LIVING

There is a particular sin that needs to be recognized and forgiven. That is the sin of burying one's talents. Cult membership is actually a cop-out from life. The proselyte who enters a cult thinks he is boldly stepping forward to commit himself wholly for the Lord's cause. In actual fact, he has unconsciously chosen a way to flee from having to make decisions, to have to stand to the consequences of free choices. He has in effect said to Moses, "Take me back to slavery. I can't stand freedom out here in the deserts of life. At least I knew how to behave there because everyone told us what to do. I didn't have to think. I only had to behave."

What has happened to him is the legal result of flight and burial—even what he thinks he has, has been taken from him (Luke 19:11–26). His freedom is forfeited. Most cults isolate their members from parents, relatives, and friends. The cult member's confidence in Christ in himself is destroyed. His ability to stand alone has been taken from him—though he surrendered it. His freedom from fear has vanished. His freedom to come and go as he wills, to meet friends, to attend parties, and to enjoy life is either radically curbed or gone altogether. In short, all the gifts of Jesus that mean abundant life have been stolen from him.

What did those have to whom more is given, and what did a cult proselyte lack that so much was taken? Trust! Those who trusted freely ventured their talents and doubled their value (vv. 16, 18). The one who lacked trust buried it for fear of loss and gave it back unchanged and consequently undeveloped and unused. That sin needs to be forgiven. Prayer ministers should make the person cognizant of the sins behind his choices, especially that of burying his talents, and should pronounce forgiveness for them.

Those delivered from cults also need healing from shame. So many we have talked with feel devastated by shame. They figure they have so blown it that they could never be used again or that God would or should never again trust them with a task. They are apt to view their entire cult experience as valueless, a prodigal journey that wasted all their Father's sustenance. They should be helped to see again that indeed all things do work together for good, that all is not lost, that they have learned valuable lessons that can be ministered as blessing to others.

Behind all the other wounds is the destruction of confidence. Praise God that all their confidence in men, and in themselves, in the flesh has been shattered. That lesson alone pays for the whole trip! To know never again to put confidence in princes is a value all the rest of the Church that idolizes pastors, leaders, and television idols could well learn from people who have freed themselves from cults. But confidence in the Lord in themselves, like trust, must be restored as a miracle gift from the Lord by prayer.

Let us praise God with them for valuable lessons learned, and then help them to learn to cherish that healthy disrespect of their own fleshly perceptions they have gained the hard way. How valuable it is to have learned so unmistakably that "there is a way which seems right to a man, but its end is the way of death" (Prov. 14:12). To have seen that one can be completely convinced of the rightness of one's own insights and yet be totally deluded is a precious safeguard for any Christian. If former cult members can be helped to see and cherish not only healthy skepticism but also to value all the other things they have learned in the wilderness, that will itself become part of their restoration of confidence. "Hey, I *have* gained something. I *am* more mature and aware by what I have been through. It wasn't all loss." But since the other side of such wilderness learning is fear and reticence, healing of the spirit is necessary to set one free.

Part of what locked cult people in was fear of failure. Being performance-oriented, they were not free to make mistakes. The essence of Christian freedom is liberty to err. Not to use that freedom as a pretext for foolishness or purposeful sin, but freedom to try things and fail. We must have confidence that our gracious and compassionate Lord has made life fun, a place in which we can try for Him. If we fail, He will turn it to glory. That aspect of confidence and trust needs to be regained. Most likely former cult members never had it in the first place. It needs to be revived from early childhood loss. Healing ought to be two-dimensional, in the present from recent devastations, and in healing of the inner man for reconstruction of trusts and freedoms that parents, by trying too hard, unwittingly demolished.

Former cult members have learned not to trust the heart of another. They have learned that even if he meant well, their leader was deluded and controlled. If he was evil, he had learned how to prey upon the naïve, good intentions of others. On one side, that also is a valuable lesson.

> Many a man proclaims his own loyalty, but who can find a trustworthy man?
>
> —PROVERBS 20:6

> Do not trust in princes, in mortal man, in whom there is no salvation.
>
> —PSALM 146:3

> It is better to take refuge in the LORD than to trust in princes.
>
> —PSALM 118:9

Those delivered from cults have learned caution the hard way. "A prudent man sees evil and hides himself, the naïve proceed and pay the penalty" (Prov. 27:12). But the continuing casualty in this case is inability to abide in friendship. They fear to risk involvement again. They need now to be taught that their experiences have so conditioned them that healed bitternesses will serve to better equip them to enter true friendship by keeping them from ever again idolizing another and consequently abdicating responsibility for their own lives. They must now learn that since no Christian should naïvely trust any other, it is only safe to trust a brother by trusting Jesus in him. Their experience has prepared them to learn true trust and friendship, to trust our Lord in another while protecting him from sinning against us by being aware and prepared to handle his propensity to sin. Our naïveté invites the worst in any brother, until maturity protects him by giving sin in him no opportunity. It is good to suspect the worst in people and draw forth their best through Christ Jesus.

Cult escapees usually have lost the gift of joy. Life has become too deadly serious for them. The childlike, which needs to live in all of us, has not only been slain, but also it is feared, because it is now identified and confused with unwanted naïveté.

But the childlike are not naïve. Childlikeness is the gift of being a child of God. I no longer have to settle problems that only He can handle. I no longer have to try to be God by solving dilemmas that are only His to solve. I can play, enjoy life, laugh at life and myself, and know that my Lord is so much Lord of life He laughs at problems and at people who persecute: "The kings of the earth take their stand, and the rulers counsel together against the LORD and against His Anointed.... He who sits in the heavens laughs, the Lord scoffs at them" (Ps. 2:2, 4). He will warn me of danger, and He will both counsel and empower my choices. He is my defense. He is responsible for me. Christians' joy is predicated upon the incontrovertible fact that the Lord *has already won the victory*. What matter any temporary setback? He will turn it to glory.

Again, however, it is not simply that these people have lost their joy. They most likely also never had it. The joy of a child is free to flourish only if parents provide security. Father and mother provide love, assurance, comfort, and safety, which in turn grant freedom to romp and play. When parents fail to provide that ambience, joy is frustrated; life becomes too serious, too soon.

Joy is native to the heart. God has created it as the natural ground of all creation. The offspring of every species in nature instinctively play, with joy! One does not have to inspire it or make it happen. One has only not to frustrate and prevent it. Therefore, prayer ministers should aim to heal until that wellspring flows unhindered again.

The key is restoration of trust. When trust in His lordship installs assurance, comfort, and safety, joy will flow naturally. We need only deal with the heart's reactions to early and recent memories and set joy free to flow.

First the Natural, Then the Supernatural

Many people who have come out of the occult fear anything supernatural. They want to immerse themselves in the good earth and forget all that spiritual stuff and junk. Who could blame them? Praise God they have learned that fools rush in where angels fear to tread. Even holy visitations of the presence of the Lord in worship services and prayer meetings may spook them. We have seen them terrorized and ready to flee when everyone else was joyfully receiving quiet anointing and blessing from the Lord. They could no longer trust their discernment, so any visitation of God frightened them. Anything beyond what the five senses could handle was too much for them. They have known goose bumps galore—and deception with it! So they fear even His presence, having lost the trust required to rest.

> Now suppose one of you fathers is asked by his son for a fish;
> he will not give him a snake instead of a fish, will he? Or if he is

asked for an egg, he will not give him a scorpion, will he? If you then, being evil, know how to give good gifts to your children, how much more shall your heavenly Father give the Holy Spirit to those who ask Him?

—LUKE 11:11–13

These scriptures lock out fear for the average Christian, but not yet for former cult members, until healing proceeds apace. It may therefore not be wisdom to subject those newly delivered from cults to high-powered services or prayer meetings. Much good human fellowship, laughter and joy, light tasks, and rest should be prescribed at first. If these people always insist on sitting near an exit, let them. If they resist touch, leave them alone. If they don't want to share vocally in a prayer meeting, don't insist that they do. The body should offer consistent warm invitation with no pressure to accept.

Many intercessory burden-bearing healing prayers, *apart from* the person, are in order. Walks in nature; good, sweaty, earthy labor; athletic exercise; good, balanced meals; abstinence from sweets; and good sleep are all healthy antidotes to the tensions in which they have lived. These people will not lose spirituality by being immersed in the good earth. They will gain it.

In J. R. R. Tolkien's trilogy, *The Lord of the Rings*, it is the hobbits, a diminutive, hardy, non-mystical, down-to-earth people, who resist the wiles of Sauron (the devil of that series) and maintain the stamina to keep going when others would drop. Tolkien makes it plain they obtain their strength from their simple earthiness, enjoying good food and fun and get-togethers as often as they can. Having been a super-spook myself, I can testify that Tolkien's grasp of reality is accurate. It is the earthy who can be safely spiritual. There is time enough after rest and earthiness for the newly delivered to return to high spiritual labors. First the natural, then the spiritual applies here (1 Cor. 15:46).

Some escapees fear demons everywhere. Some were taught to look for them in everyone—and of course they saw what they looked for, whether they were there or not. Dr. Bill Johnson, a Spirit-filled believer who was head of psychology at Whitworth College, once said that although psychology can't bring full healing, it can chronicle the deceits of the flesh. When the leader of a cult movement took over the headship in his church, the congregation was told from the pulpit that anyone who had anything to do with psychology was filled with demons! Those false teachers saw demons in everything and everyone. Of course, they were the only ones not possessed, and therefore proximity to them became the only safe place to dwell! Fear of demons thus slammed the prison doors shut for all who believed the false perceptions of the cult leaders.

Many Christians, lacking the wisdom of the deprogrammers of whom we spoke, have thought to shout demons out of cult people, trying to set them free. That memory may also be part of what makes them continue to remain skittish and fearful. Such people need time and earthiness in order to appreciate again that "this is simply this" and "that is simply that," and not everything is fraught with demons.

We urge prayer ministers to be cautious about doing exorcisms either on or in the presence of ex-cult members. If demons do indeed bother them, let us bind them silently and wait awhile. There is no hurry. Time is on our side. The person is moving into more and more light; he is becoming stronger day by day. If a prayer minister leads into healing inner wounds and so sets the person free, demons lose power to entrap their intended victims in trouble again. The possible presence of a demon does not dictate immediate exorcism. Our Lord does, in His own time and wisdom.

TRANSFORMING RELATIONSHIPS

Reconciliation to family and friends eventually is in order. Sometimes that should be postponed, when one sees that the overbearing or angry or critical nature of family members would harm more than help. Usually, however, the sooner, the better. Family and friends can be prepared for reunion by being advised not to scold or to ask too many questions too soon. Family members should be instructed to express affection and gratitude to have the cult member home again, and to be as natural and open as the heightened emotions of the moment will allow. Family should not overdo and make the ex-cult member feel like a pampered guest. That says, "You're not home yet, and we know it." Old routines and chores have a tonic effect when we come out of the bizarre into the home again.

Whisperings behind the back will most likely be noticed. Awkwardness is to be expected. It would be the same were he only coming home from war or a long stay in college. Just weather it. He wants to be treated like anyone else, not as special or different.

Former cult members may want to talk. Family members should let them, but be instructed to view most of it as cathartic, a mere need to get things off the chest. The former cult member should not be taught, scolded, or counseled by his family, or anything else than merely heard and understood. Most returnees lapse into silence rather than talk too much. It helps to allow some withdrawal but prevent too much by drawing the person into family events, like picnics, ball games, fun around the table, and so forth.

Most of all, the family should not be isolated. Continued contact with and advice from counselors, prayer ministers, or deprogrammers is nearly a must. Situations will arise in which parents and relatives have no idea what is the wise way to act, or how the ex-cult son or daughter most likely will be affected. That is why we are a church rather than solitary pilgrims. Wise parents and friends will avail themselves of counsel.

Heart-to-heart talks with the father and mother are extremely desirable. Most parents would be well advised to undergo some prayer ministry themselves before that opportunity presents itself. Even if a father thinks he has no problems and doesn't require ministry for himself, going through it will build into him an awareness that will stand him in good stead when his son or daughter comes to talk. Self-awareness normally grows by leaps and bounds under ministry, whereas most parents, without undergoing ministry, usually shoot down their position with their children by remaining too unaware how what they say or do affects the young person. Especially, a father or mother needs to be helped to see how the family members' lifestyles affected or afflicted the son or daughter and caused or helped to create the weaknesses by which the child became enmeshed in the cult. Prayer ministry will also help the parents to confess their own faults to the child and to ask forgiveness rather than self-righteously blaming their son or daughter for falling.

Finally, former cult members need somewhere to lay the shoulder to the wheel, somewhere to find wholeness by contributing in a worthwhile way. Perhaps after a time of rest a good job can be found, or some form of ministry. Nazi scientists who were so under the spell of Nazism that they brutally used slave labor and caused horrible deaths to thousands were so shocked and overwhelmed with guilt when the evil cloud lifted that many of them poured themselves unremittingly into efforts to contribute their knowledge to good causes. All redeemed persons want to serve somewhere to make amends. It is especially tonic to cult escapees, for it also helps to restore confidence in themselves by once again being part of an ongoing society. Cults catch hold of the immature at the point of rebellion. All of society is to them "establishment" and evil, and they think they must go to opposite extremes to stand against it. Cults seem to offer a "holy" corrective, like the only ten righteous who could save the city of Sodom. Once delivered, the former cult member says, "I now want to contribute to the society I once despised. Let me work. By doing so, I enter the stream of life and learn at last to accept the unworkable and the imperfect within it."

The end result of freedom from cults should be maturity. If the person remains naïve and frightened, something hasn't happened. More prayer ministry is needed. Persons free from cult experience should be given, when ready, the robe of ruling, the ring of authority, and the fatted calf of celebration. Who knows better than these returned prodigals the pitfalls of faith? Who has learned more intensely than they to abide in Jesus and put no trust in men? As men continue to wander into humanism, as homes continue to fracture more and more, religious cults and political demagoguery will increase. We shall need the experience and consequent wisdom of those who have been there and back again. In the meantime, let us not treat them as second-class Christians. They will have become wise and chastened when prayer ministry has winnowed the wheat, kept the kernels, and blown away the chaff.

EFFECTS FROM OUR SIN-SICKENED CULTURE

T HERE IS NO DENYING the fact that we live in a sin-sickened culture today. Defilement comes into our minds, and so into our spirits, through all the various media—education, news, television, movies, novels, video games, Internet influences, and so forth.

There is little need to document the miasma of false examples and teachings that flow through every form of the media. "And the serpent poured water like a river *out of his mouth* after the woman, so that he might cause her to be swept away with the flood" (Rev. 12:15, emphasis added). Whatever else that may mean, it certainly is a vivid description of the movies, music, Hollywood stars, drugs, false teachings of the media, and so forth, ad nauseam, that have flooded onto our heads like an unceasing Niagara. Surely its aim is to sweep away the woman and us! Regrettably, we have heard of hundreds of cases of Christians who are living together in sin, outside the sanctity of marriage, who have bought the lie that love makes it all right—"and anyway, everybody's doing it these days." Christian singles groups are all too frequently full of those who praise God on Sundays and fornicate all week! What would have been rated "X" a generation ago is now unthinkingly accepted as "PG." Almost every hero figure in movies, television, and novels is portrayed as thinking nothing of hopping into bed with anyone, anytime. When 007 has intercourse with every heroine and villainness, that's bad enough, but now hospital head surgeons, police chiefs, and every other kind of hero are explicitly portrayed as having the same kind of illicit love affairs! Movies make champions of thieves and induce vast audiences to hope they escape scot-free. And there is no end in sight.

The battle is on for the control of men's minds. In this warfare, believers need to pray that their spirits will be cleansed and awakened. Believers need to intercede for others. In the end, however, each man will have to fight his own mind's battle. The antidote is simple. There is no other or no better solution than settling it once and for all in the mind, in the will, and in the heart that God's laws, expressed in His Word, are absolute!

Today there is little or no proper fear of God. "The fear of the LORD is the beginning of wisdom, and the knowledge of the Holy One is understanding" (Prov. 9:10). But how shall we regain true fear of God for ourselves and for our people? The crux of this conclusion depends upon you, the reader, comprehending what makes the difference between those who determine to believe the laws of God but who, when the pressures are on, cannot remember or persist, and those who make the same determination and truly can live by it. The telling factor is one thing only. Some have a root, and some do not: "And those on the rocky soil are those who, when they hear, receive the word with joy; *and these have no firm root*; they believe for a while, and in time of temptation fall away" (Luke 8:13, emphasis added).

What is it to have a root? How do we get one? Roots reach into the soil and drink nurture. Roots must have good soil, or their plants starve. Roots must reach to water, or their plants wither. Parental affection, love, acceptance, security, and discipline are the ground from which children's roots drink nurture. Their roots are their family and heritage, but it is their spirits that reach beyond their bodies into the fertile soil of affection and acceptance to drink strength in the spirit, first from their parents, and then, by that enabling, from God.

As children drink nurture through their roots by their spirits, they learn respect, admiration, and trust. When awareness of God comes, those qualities become awe and reverence, which become true fear of God. True fear of God is birthed and housed in the life of our personal spirits, or not at all. Children who do not receive sufficient nurture have slumbering spirits. Their hearts are rocky soil, and they have no awakened spirit to push through its crags and fractures to find footing and nurture in love and affection in God or in mankind. Thus they have no root. Mental determination and willpower are not enough. The conscience does not work in children with no root, because their spirit fails to function. Therefore they fall in time of temptation.

Preachers may blast away at the onrushing flood of our culture and exhort manfully—and fail miserably—until they realize that unless their people have viable roots, they cannot stand! How then shall we settle it once and for all that God's law is absolute? Not by fleshly willpower. That won't work. Not by screwing up our determination to believe. We hear much about "faith" today, but often it seems merely a catchword with little or no real content. Faith is relationship. It is real, undeniable, constantly experienced relationship with God. The only way we can travel that distance from head knowledge to true faith "rooted and grounded in love" (Eph. 3:17) is to obtain a functioning root system by reviving and awakening the personal spirit of each person!

In the beginning of our ministry, I tried to do something about the flood of pornography that was even then beginning to sweep across the land. Learning of the organization "Citizens for Decent Literature" (CDL), I stumped through every civic body where I could wangle an invitation to speak in Streator, Illinois, warning of danger, calling for belief, and enlisting citizens in CDL. In the end we had over fifty clubs and societies involved, and hundreds of alerted citizens. The only fruit I could see that resulted from all that effort was that more people bought smutty magazines and streamed to risqué movies! They wanted to know what they were being told to be against! It was as though, like the Roman Catholic Church of long ago, I had banned books only to make sure everyone ran right out to buy one!

Prohibition of alcohol made millionaires of black marketeers and entrenched the Mafia in America. I learned the hard way that preaching and teaching against evil will only publicize and spread it. Not that we should not do so occasionally. Once in a while alerts our people to danger. But constant trumpeting produces drastically reversed returns. *It is the preaching of good news that has power!* Only as true faith is birthed and spirits awaken do men truly stand!

Not knowing or understanding this, too many pastors weary themselves trying to stamp out brush fires of sin until the Lord returns, and have as little lasting effect as tumbleweeds blown across the land! Please hear it again. *Only* as men gain true rootage in Him do they have power to stand. Much of our effort today reminds me of those birthday candles designed to reignite after being blown out. We huff and puff at sin, only to see it flame up again as soon as we turn to the next subject.

Hear again the prophecy of Malachi 4:5–6:

> Behold, I am going to send you Elijah the prophet before the coming of the great and terrible day of the LORD. And he will restore the hearts of the fathers to their children, and the hearts of the children to their fathers, lest I come and smite the land with a curse.

Only as fathers' hearts are turned to their children, and vice versa, will children's hearts be rooted and grounded in love. Only then will spirits truly be rooted in the fear of God. Only then will lives have strength of spirit to "put on the full armor of God, that you may be able to stand firm against the schemes of the devil...and having done everything, to stand firm" (Eph. 6:11, 13). Do pastors want to give their congregations ability to stand, holy and strong? Let them work to restore their families! Let them heal the hearts of the wounded and revive and awaken the slumbering. Just so, and only so, will men truly believe and stand to His Word.

Truly each man must make his own decision and determine to stand. But hollow men cannot stand. We must give them the equipment. We must set their spirits free from stupor. Once men's spirits are awakened, righteousness will roll down like a mighty river, and men's outraged spirits will no longer tolerate the evils we now only mildly deplore. Healing of wounded and slumbering spirits is the only viable key to rearming a moral society. Let's get at it!

NOTES

Chapter 3
Performance Orientation

1. Erich Fromm, *The Fear of Freedom* (London: Routledge and Kegan Paul, 1960).

Chapter 4
The Base of Law

1. Karl Menninger, *Whatever Became of Sin?* (New York: Hawthorn Books, 1973).

Chapter 5
The Central Power and
Necessity of Forgiveness

1. "I Am Thine, O Lord" by Fanny J. Crosby. Public domain.

CHAPTER 6
BREAKING THE CYCLE

1. Belly is rendered "from within him" (ASV and NIV), "heart" (RSV), and "innermost being" (NAS, footnote, "literally, *out of his belly*").

CHAPTER 7
THE ROLE OF A PRAYER MINISTER

1. U.S. Catholic Church, *Catechism of the Catholic Church*, second edition (New York: Doubleday, 2003), 402.

CHAPTER 9
GENERATIONAL SIN

1. Barbara Shlemon Ryan, *Healing Prayer* (Ann Arbor, MI: Charis Books, 2001).

OTHER BOOKS by JOHN and PAULA SANDFORD

A Comprehensive Guide to Deliverance and Inner Healing

Awakening the Slumbering Spirit

Choosing Forgiveness

Elijah Among Us

God's Power to Change

Healing for a Woman's Emotions

Healing the Nations

Healing Victims of Sexual Abuse

Prophets, Healers and the Emerging Church

Renewal of the Mind

Restoring the Christian Family

The Elijah Task

Why Good People Mess Up

For further information, contact:

Elijah House Ministries
317 N. Pines Road
Spokane Valley, WA 99206
Web site: www.elijahhouse.org

JOHN LOREN and PAULA SANDFORD

have devoted their lives to helping people make changes and walk out their victories.

978-1-59979-020-6 / $14.99

We pray that God has been revealed in *Transforming the Inner Man*. Here is another classic teaching from John and Paula Sandford.

The Elijah Task

It is time to see the task God has set before you!

For prophets and intercessors who want a deeper understanding of their role in the world today (and for those who want to understand and support the prophets and intercessors), all of you have a mighty important job to do.

The spirit of Elijah is repentance, which brings change and great joy! There is much work to be done, and *The Elijah Task* is the perfect place to start.

Visit your local bookstore today.

FREE NEWSLETTERS
TO HELP EMPOWER YOUR LIFE

Why subscribe today?

☐ **DELIVERED DIRECTLY TO YOU.** All you have to do is open your inbox and read.

☐ **EXCLUSIVE CONTENT.** We cover the news overlooked by the mainstream press.

☐ **STAY CURRENT.** Find the latest court rulings, revivals, and cultural trends.

☐ **UPDATE OTHERS.** Easy to forward to friends and family with the click of your mouse.

CHOOSE THE E-NEWSLETTER THAT INTERESTS YOU MOST:

- Christian news
- Daily devotionals
- Spiritual empowerment
- And much, much more

SIGN UP AT: **http://freenewsletters.charismamag.com**